The History of Nassau County Community Place-Names

Richard A. Winsche

A Long Island Studies Institute Publication
from
HOFSTRA UNIVERSITY

Empire State Books
Interlaken, New York
1999

A *quality* publication from
Heart of the Lakes Publishing
Interlaken, New York 14847

Dedication

To my brother Jack

and

The memory of our parents

Map of Nassau County, 1990 showing Cities, Villages and Communities

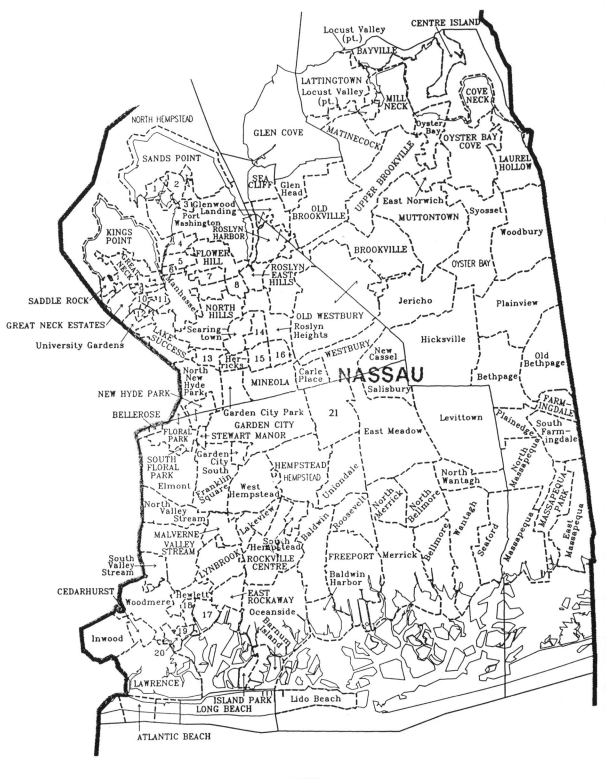

KEY

1 MANORHAVEN	8 ROSLYN ESTATES	15 WILISTON PARK
2 PORT WASHINGTON	9 KENSINGTON	16 EAST WILLISTON
3 BAXTER ESTATES	10 GREAT NECK PLAZA	17 HEWLETT HARBOR
4 PLANDOME MANOR	11 THOMASTON	18 HEWLETT BAY PARK
5 PLANDOME	12 RUSSELL GARDENS	19 HEWLETT NECK
6 PLANDOME HEIGHTS	13 Manhasset Hills	20 WOODSBURGH
7 MUNSEY PARK	14 Albertson	21 East Garden City

Contents

On facing page:
Map of Nassau County, 1990.
Source: *1990 Census of Population and Housing, New York* (Washington, DC: Bureau of the Census, 1991), CPH-2-34, G-11. The numbers in the key refer to communities whose area is too small to have their names on the map. Places in all capital letters are incorporated cities and villages.

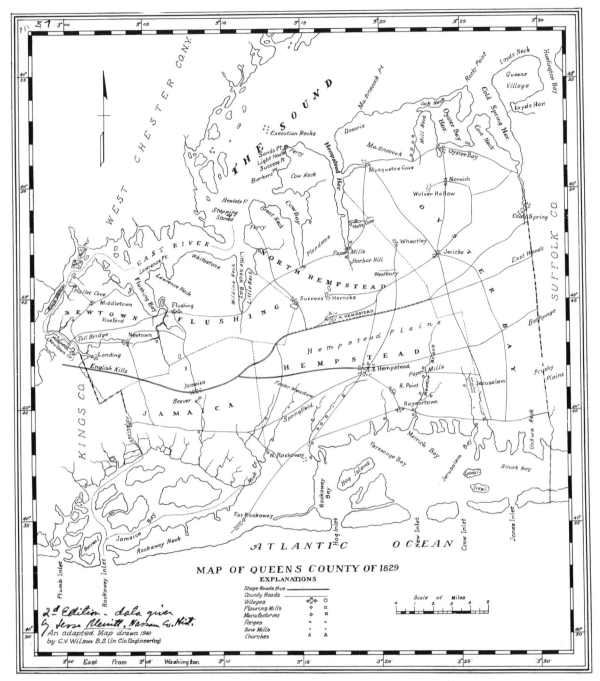

Queens County, 1829, showing villages, towns, churches, roads, and mills. Lloyd Harbor ("Queens Village") then was part of the Town of Oyster Bay and the Rockaway Peninsula (or Rockaway Neck), part of the Town of Hempstead. This map was drawn c. 1940. Copy in the Nassau County Museum collection, Long Island Studies Institute at Hofstra University.

Foreword

The origins of place-names and histories of local communities have a continuing fascination. "Locality," it has been argued, "is truly the only reality," and it is only by understanding the history of a community that we can understand ourselves.[1] One of the critical starting points in any local history is the origin of the name of the community. George R. Stewart has written classic accounts for many communities, and local researchers have studied some Long Island place-names.[2] None of these, however, has provided as extensive and detailed study of Long Island place-names as Richard A. Winsche's research on Nassau County communities.

This book has its origins in Winsche's Master's thesis at the Graduate Faculties of Long Island University (C. W. Post College) three decades ago.[3] Over the years since that time he has continued his interest in the topic and collected further information on the history of place-names. Now, in his retirement years, he has had an opportunity to integrate his many years of research on the topic, update his original work, and reorganize his material. The Long Island Studies Institute is honored to be able to publish this important reference work in Nassau County's centennial year.

Richard A. Winsche has searched the town records for the earliest use of place-names and investigated the origins of those names. An indefatigable newspaper researcher, he has pored over hundreds of reels of newspapers on microfilm to locate articles on the naming of communities. (A list of the newspapers covered follows the bibliography.)[4] Whenever possible, he has included references to a contemporary account of who suggested a name and why, as well as any other names proposed and attempts to change the name. Moreover, he contacted clerks of the incorporated villages to ascertain the dates of incorporation. This volume is the culmination of his work. To make the information easily accessible, entries and notes are arranged alphabetically by community. To lead researchers to other sources, we have added titles of other histories of the places when they are available.

Some of the names of communities are derived from Native American designations. Scholars today indicate that the traditional "tribal names" which the European settlers associated with Long Island's Indians are the Algonquian descriptions of the geographical features of the area rather than their own names for themselves. William Wallace Tooker extensively investigated Long Island Indian place-names at the turn of the last century. He was handicapped because the Algonquian language spoken by the Indians here had virtually disappeared, with only minimal records of names.[5] Although Tooker's accuracy of the meaning of various Indian words has been questioned by modern scholars, his translations are the best we have and, appropriately, are relied upon in this account. These Algonquian names have many variations in spelling. Quotations from town records have followed the original. In the colonial period, spelling was often phonetic and not standardized. If you do not recognize a word, say it aloud, and you should recognize it by the sound.[6]

The post office often had an important role in the naming of communities. The United States postal service would not establish a post office in a community which wanted to use the same name as another community in the state. This resulted in such changes as *New* Hyde Park and Cold Spring *Harbor* to distinguish from upstate communities. As Winsche's research indicates, sometimes a community was named after early settlers, the place from which they migrated, or from geographical features. Quakers often adopted biblical names for their communities. The Long Island Rail Road, in naming its stations, also was a significant influence on place-names. In other communities, individual or corporate developers and realtors originated the name of the community.

Some background on political and geographical designations may be helpful. Nassau County was organized in 1899, after the three western towns of Queens (and the Rockaway peninsula of the Town of Hempstead) became part of greater New York City.[7] Nassau County has two cities (Glen Cove and Long Beach), three towns (Hempstead, North Hempstead, and Oyster Bay), sixty-four incorporated villages, and more than fifty other communities—hamlets or "census designated places" (unincorporated areas within the town). A few communities straddle town or county lines. School districts and postal zones are not necessarily identical with villages or communities bearing the same name. Neighborhoods are informal geographical areas without official boundaries. The place-names discussed here are incorporated villages and communities with recognizable boundaries. Following common usage, they are often referred to as villages, but the author has capitalized village in references to the incorporated villages to differentiate them.[8]

In the 1920s, many estate owners joined together to incorporate as villages to secure local political control. This resulted in the creation of many "estate villages" that were quite small in population. Incorporation enabled the estate owners to avoid special district taxes for public improvements and to control local roads, parking, and development in their "golf club" villages. In 1932, New York State enacted legislation requiring a minimum population of 500 for incorporation as a village, effectively ending the creation of estate villages. Furthermore, many suburban communities in Nassau County (and throughout New York State) utilized town improvement districts to provide services. When Nassau County adopted its new charter in 1938, the charter reserved zoning rights to the towns for any future villages. This ended the major incentive for the creation of incorporated villages. The only incorporated village in Nassau County created since 1932 is Atlantic Beach (1962).[9]

Hempstead is the oldest village in Nassau, both in terms of initial settlement (1643-1644) and incorporation (1853). When Nassau County was formed in 1899, the county's population was about 55,000. Other incorporated villages were Sea Cliff, a camp meeting ground and summer resort (incorporated in 1883), Freeport (1892), Rockville Centre (1893), and Lawrence (1897). In the first decade of the twentieth century, East Rockaway, Farmingdale, Mineola, and Floral Park were incorporated. Fourteen villages were incorporated between 1910 and 1920. The boom years for incorporation were the 1920s and early 1930s, when forty-six villages and two cities were incorporated. Many of these communities were undergoing population growth and wanted to secure local improvements and services such as waste disposal, street paving, fire and police protection, and street lights. Such estate villages as Centre Island, Cove Neck, and Saddle Rock typically had small populations and were created by the principal landowners to maintain their exclusiveness and control development.

Those researching the history of a specific community should first investigate the resources of the local library for the locality. The extent of resources varies for different communities and libraries. The Bryant Library in Roslyn and the Glen Cove Library, for example, have excellent local history collections. Elly Shodell, at the Port Washington Library, has conducted an extensive oral history program documenting that community's history. Historical societies, preservation groups, and local historians may also have valuable resources.[10] Obviously not all of these 115 communities have their own libraries, but some of the fifty-four public libraries in Nassau County cover a broader area. Local histories may also extend beyond one community. Cross references in the notes for the Five Towns communities indicate this explicitly, but histories of Great Neck may cover the numerous incorporated villages on the peninsula. This is true also for Port Washington and Manhasset, as well as neighboring communities. The derivation of place-names for communities which share a name (e.g. Hempstead and West Hempstead) will also share the history of that name. In some cases information has been repeated, but readers are advised to consult all entries with the community's name. The index lists all places mentioned, including former names and names proposed but not adopted, as well as the names of all people in the text.

The Appendix lists population figures for each community for 1990 and the most recent estimated population (1998), as well as area and population density.[11] The bibliography includes all books and articles cited in the notes.

This and other Institute publications are made possible through the support of Hofstra University and the commitment of its president, James M. Shuart, to the Long Island Studies Institute. Victoria Aspinwall, secretary for the Long Island Studies Institute, entered the manuscript on the computer, created the bibliography from the entries in the notes, calculated population densities for the appendix, proofread, and indexed the volume. Dorothy B. Ruettgers assisted in copy editing the volume. Richard Winsche, in addition to having done the prodigious research, aided in proofreading the text and compiling the index. Walter Steesy of Heart of the Lakes/Empire State Books has provided helpful assistance in the publishing process.

Natalie A. Naylor, Director
Long Island Studies Institute

Preface

During the years I served as Historian for the Nassau County Division of Museum Services many inquiries were received asking when and why a particular village was so named. In attempting to answer these questions, it became apparent that accurate information in this area was often lacking. For this reason, I began research on this subject, and it became the basis for my master's thesis, where much of this material originally appeared. I have updated and reorganized the material for this publication.

Future research will shed further enlightenment on the subject of the origin and history of Nassau County village place-names. I hope that when additional information is discovered, not too many errors will be found to have appeared in this work. For those which may have inadvertently found their way to these pages, I accept complete responsibility.

For their assistance, I wish to thank a number of individuals. Foremost among them is Vincent F. Seyfried, that great researcher, whose writings were of inestimable value; John A. Hewlett, the late Peter Luyster Van Santvoord, and Gary R. Hammond, former co-workers with the Nassau County Museum System, who guided me in discovering valuable sources of information; Edward J. Smits, Nassau County Historian, for his encouragement; Dr. Myron H. Luke, dean of Long Island historians, and the late Dr. Kenneth Colegrove, who served on my master's committee and led me in the right direction; Dorothy V. Reinhard for typing the original draft of this work, Victoria Aspinwall for retyping it; and finally, Dr. Natalie A. Naylor, editor of this volume, for her generous assistance.

Introduction

Generally Nassau County village place-names may be placed in one of five different categories. There are those named for the Indian tribe or chieftaincy which had inhabited the area or some aboriginal name or word that was felt to be significant. Some names were taken from the place from which the original settlers had come, or from the Bible. Other names are descriptive of the area. Some communities were named for an individual or family that usually had some importance to the history of the village. Finally, there are those which were selected because they had a pleasant or euphonious sound.

In examining aboriginal place-names it became obvious that the residents of Nassau County felt no obligation to preserve these designations. Of those names still in existence, only East Rockaway and Merrick can be said to have been in continuous use since those areas were first settled. All other aboriginal place-names now being used were resurrected from the past. In several cases these appellations were erroneous when applied to a particular village or locality. Generally, however, when fully understood the aboriginal names were distinguished by their propriety and suitability and it is to be regretted that many were not preserved. The etymology of aboriginal place-names in this study has relied upon such works as *Aboriginal Place-Names of New York,* by William M. Beauchamp; *Indian Names of Long Island Localities,* by James Ellsworth DeKay; and *The Indian Place-Names of Long Island,* by William Wallace Tooker.[1] While recent scholars have questioned portions of those pioneers' works, they have offered nothing substantial in the way of a replacement.

This study will show that the residents of many of Nassau County's villages adopted names for their communities which had originally been used in other areas. Usually those names were taken from the village or area from which the settlers had migrated or which had some other historic connection. Also, a number of place-names were taken from the Bible. These generally appear to have been used in areas which were primarily populated by Quakers who, because of their strong religious beliefs, were drawn to the Bible in selecting names for their villages.

A majority of the personal place-names in Nassau County commemorate persons who were important in shaping the history of their communities. They were often the original settlers of the areas which now bear their names, or they contributed in some way to the development and growth of these localities. On occasion, attempts were made to change the names of some of these villages, but the residents fought those efforts, and these appellations were preserved.

Many villages received their names because they described some feature of the community or locality. Fortunately, even some of the newer names that have been adopted, such as Atlantic Beach and East Hills, appropriately describe the areas to which they were given. Others, such as Island Trees and Muttontown, have lost the element which caused them to be descriptive in nature. When the meaning of those names is understood, however, their historic value becomes obvious, and it is hoped they will always be preserved.

Only a small percentage of Nassau County village place-names are euphonious in nature. Designations of this type are of little value in interpreting the history of the villages, as these names were often given by real estate developers in the hope of attracting new residents. Many of these village names may be said to have acquired some degree of historic value, or at least antiquity, through the passage of time and are valued by the inhabitants of those communities.

Research for this work required consulting all the general Long Island and village histories, but it was discovered that they often were lacking information relating to place-names, or in some instances, the information they contained was erroneous. For this reason it became necessary to turn to local newspapers as a source. Contemporary newspapers may be considered a primary source if there is no contradictory evidence and their statement seems to be credible or conclusive. As has been stated: "The chief mine of information for writing local history is in the files of old newspapers."[2] This has proven to be especially true in place-name research, where much of the information so contained was not considered important enough to include in other works.

When possible, this study provides the date that a village or locality was settled. It indicates when the present place-name came into use and also gives a chronology of the names which may have preceded this designation. In addition, an attempt has been made to identify the person who may have suggested a particular name and the reason this was done. This material is supplemented with information regarding any known attempts to change present village names. In designating the various villages, the word village is capitalized only when referring to those which are incorporated, e.g., the Village of Atlantic Beach. In determining which communities should be a part of this work, all recognized villages, as well as those localities which had post offices, school districts, and other distinctive features, were included. Sources used in making this determination were the index to municipalities and localities in *Hagstrom Nassau County Atlas,* 1992; *Long Island, The Sunrise Homeland, 1957;* the *Nassau County, New York, Data Book,* 1985; and the *Long Island Gazetteer,* 1984.[3]

Albertson

Although members of the Albertson family had settled in Nassau County as early as 1687, they did not arrive in the area now bearing their name until the middle of the nineteenth century.[1] In the early 1800s, Benjamin Albertson acquired land in Mineola at the intersection of Roslyn Road and Old Country Road and established a farm there. This property was to be inherited by his son, Thomas W. Albertson, who farmed this property and also was noted as an inventor.[2] He devised a unique wind gristmill which was erected on that property and remained there until all the buildings were demolished in the late 1950s.

In addition to that property, Benjamin Albertson had also acquired land some distance to the north in what was to become the village of Albertson. Following his death, it was deeded to his son, Richard Albertson, by his wife and the other children on March 5, 1845.[3] This farm originally consisted of fifty acres of land and was enlarged by Richard Albertson through additional purchases until it contained more than 150 acres. By the 1860s, he was the largest landholder in that area. When the Locust Valley branch of the railroad was constructed in 1863-1864, it passed through his property.[4]

On November 9, 1874, Richard Albertson sold this property to his nephew, Townsend Albertson, for $21,000.[5] Several sources have stated that the area was then named for Townsend Albertson, but this is in error.[6] Actually, the name Albertson seems to have been given by the Long Island Rail Road, which established a stop there with that designation in March 1874, some eight months before Townsend Albertson took possession of his uncle's farm.[7] Whether the railroad honored Richard Albertson by naming this stop after him because he gave them property for the right-of-way, or simply because he was the largest land owner in the area, is unknown.

Because the name Albertson was being used by the railroad, it came into general use as the designation for the area and the village which eventually grew there.

Atlantic Beach

The history and name of the Village of Atlantic Beach was the same as that of Long Beach until the development of this community was begun. The first reference to the appellation Atlantic Beach occurred on February 1, 1889, when a local newspaper reported that: "A certificate of incorporation of the Atlantic Beach Company was filed with the Secretary of State. Its operations are to be carried on in the town of Hempstead. Its objects are the purchasing of real estate and buildings, and settling and improving the same. . . . The trustees are Robert Colwell, Thos. B. Inness and Chas. B. Kaufman."[1]

Apparently this company failed, and both the development and name of Atlantic Beach fell into obscurity for a number of years. Following World War I, however, a new attempt to promote this locality was begun. At this time Stephen P. Pettit, in partnership with T. Benson Smith, formed a company which proposed to handle real estate developments and sales. In addition to developing sections of Baldwin, Bellmore, and Valley Stream, this company also acquired the rights to the Atlantic Beach area.[2]

Because of its geographical location by the Atlantic Ocean on Long Beach island, Pettit re-adopted the very descriptive designation of Atlantic Beach as the name of this area.[3] In a biographical sketch of Pettit written in 1925, it was stated that:

> Perhaps one of the most important and spectacular achievements of this concern is at Atlantic Beach, where they have developed three thousand five hundred lots along the ocean front between Long Beach and Rockaway. There extensive improvements have already been constructed and many cottages have been erected.[4]

Before further development of the area could be accomplished, Pettit died and the holdings of the Atlantic Beach Associates, Inc., were sold. At the time of this sale it was reported that:

> Steve Pettit's dream is about to come true. The vision of the former sheriff and politician of a great high-class resort by the sea, at the westerly end of Long Beach will soon be realized. Atlantic Beach, his creation and on which more than $1,000,000 already has been spent, has been sold to Island Park Associates, headed by L. M. Austin, Jr., and C. N. Talbot, for upwards of $4,000,000. . . .
>
> Atlantic Beach, with more than a mile and a half of ocean front and two miles along the inlet, is the last remaining large piece available close to the city for a great ocean resort.[5]

Although this last venture was successful, it was not until June 2, 1962, that this village was officially incorporated under the name of Atlantic Beach. It was the last village to be incorporated in Nassau County.[6]

Baldwin

The name Baldwin is the last of a series of appellations which were applied to the area located immediately to the west of Freeport. The Town Records first refer to this locality as "Hicks his Neck," in a deed dated July 12, 1671.[1] This name became transposed to Hick's Neck and continued to be used until the late 1700s. The reason this designation was adopted was because John Hicks was one of the first settlers in the area.[2]

In 1810, the first church in this emerging village was built. This church was known as Bethel Chapel, and eventually a portion of the village near the church received the name Bethel. Shortly after the Revolutionary War, however, the village proper began to be referred to as Milburn Corners.[3] This name was taken from Milburn Creek, which ran from the bay into the southern part of the village.

Thomas Baldwin purchased land on Merrick Road in this village in 1825, and erected a hotel which became known as the Baldwin House. He also owned and operated a general store known as T. Baldwin and Sons, and because of his importance in the village, it became known as Baldwinville.[4] This name was used until July 1868, when it was announced that the designation of the railroad station there had been changed to Fox Borough. This new name had been adopted to honor Charles Fox, President of the South Side Rail Road of Long Island.[5]

The newspaper which reported the adoption of Fox Borough as the new name stated: "Some people do not see the necessity of a change of name; but it should be borne in mind that there is a Baldwinsville P.O. in Onondaga county, in this state." Apparently this statement annoyed some of the village's residents who stated that the name of their village was Baldwinville and not Baldwinsville. It was also announced that the post master was refusing to accept any letters or packages which were addressed to Fox Borough.[6]

This dispute over the name of the village, post office, and railroad station was resolved in 1869, when all were again united under the name of Baldwinville.[7] At this time the name was chosen to honor Francis B. Baldwin, Thomas Baldwin's son, who was a prominent New York City merchant and who had served as Treasurer of Queens County.[8]

In July 1872, the name was again changed when it was shortened to Baldwins.[9] This designation was used until January 1892, when Austin Corbin, President of the Long Island Rail Road, decided to remove what he termed proprietary names from all railroad stations. He had a petition left at the Baldwins station for the purpose of learning how many people would be in favor of changing the designation of that station to Milburn. Despite the fact that only twelve people signed this petition, the name of the station was changed on February 1, 1892.[10]

The residents of the village resented this action and refused to change the name of their post office, which remained Baldwins. A local newspaper stated, "The post office bears a name sign with the legend 'Post Office, Baldwins,' in letters so large 'that he who runs may read.'" Despite this militant stand in retaining the designation of Baldwins as the name of the post office, it was announced in August 1895, that it would also be changed to Milburn.[11] This change was never made, however, because the village's residents were still opposed to the move.

In June 1897, after the death of Austin Corbin, the Long Island Rail Road stated that thereafter all depots would have the same name as the villages' post offices, to end any confusion which may have been caused by the duplication of names. Therefore, on June 17, 1897, the name of the railroad station in that village again became known as Baldwins. The final change of appellations occurred in November 1900, when Baldwins was shortened to simply Baldwin.[12]

This name has endured to this day with no further attempts to change it. In 1925, however, there was great controversy over whether the village should become incorporated. When the proposal was defeated, some of the backers of David V. Dailey, a leader in the movement, suggested that the section of the village he represented be incorporated under the name of Daileyville.[13] This idea, however, was never seriously considered by the majority of the area's residents, and eventually it was abandoned.[14]

A section of the village of Baldwin, located on Baldwin Bay, became known as Baldwin Harbor when it was developed in the early 1900s. This area, however, is merely a portion of the village of Baldwin and has no officially recognized independent existence.

Baxter Estates

The Village of Baxter Estates, which adjoins the much larger area of Port Washington, was originally known as a part of Cow Neck. This designation, which first appears in the Town Records on April 23, 1669, referred to the peninsula of that name.[1] It was adopted because, with the addition of a fence across its base, it was a natural pasture for the cattle owned by the Town's residents. This peninsula eventually became known as Manhasset Neck, and this name has prevailed. The Baxter Estates area, however, was most closely connected to its neighbor, Port Washington. Like that village, it was generally referred to as Cow Bay and, after 1859, as Port Washington.[2]

The first mention of the Baxter family, for whom this village was to be named, appeared in the Town Records on April 28, 1743, when Oliver Baxter purchased land in the Port Washington area. From this date through the early 1900s, the Baxters were one of the most influential families in that locality. By the late 1890s, they had acquired large land holdings in the area that was to become the Village of Baxter Estates.[3]

In 1907, Allen P. Baxter, a lawyer who was born in this area, entered the real estate business in partnership with Charles E. Hyde. Hyde, who was also from Port Washington, had previously engaged in a number of occupations before he opened his own real estate agency in 1895.[4] In May 1910, Baxter and Hyde joined with Isaac A. Willets and H. Richard Morris to form a corporation known as Baxter Estates Incorporated.[5] They then began developing the area which was to become the Village of Baxter Estates, which they so named because the property had long been owned by the Baxter family. By 1914, this area had acquired an identity separate from Port Washington and was already known by its new name.[6]

In 1931, the residents of Baxter Estates became concerned over the possibility that Port Washington would become an incorporated village and annex their area.[7] To prevent this and retain their independence, the residents of Baxter Estates took the initiative and incorporated their village. Ironically, the village of Port Washington did not incorporate, so their independence was never actually threatened.

Bay Park

The village of Bay Park was associated with and was a part of East Rockaway until 1912. For that reason it was originally referred to as Near Rockaway, and when that village changed its name, it became known as a part of East Rockaway. In 1912, however, the East Rockaway Civic Association published a booklet that contained an advertisement of the Windsor Land and Improvement Company that stated: "Their new development at East Rockaway, on Hewlett's Bay, will be the greatest on modern Long Island. More than $100,000 will be expended in dredging the Yacht Harbor and surface improvements on the land. It is proposed to make this section of suburban Long Island surpass anything on the south shore within commuting distance of New York."[1]

At the time this original attempt was made to develop this locality, it was known as East Rockaway Park.[2] The Windsor Land and Development Company, however, realized that if it were to promote this area, it would need a more appealing designation. For this reason they selected the name Bay Park, as it was felt to be euphonious and descriptive of this area, which was bounded on the south and east by Hewlett Bay, and on the west by Hewlett Point Park.[3]

In 1914, what became known as the Grand Canal was dredged and bulk-headed, but World War I prevented further improvements from being made at that time. Following the war this property was acquired by Realty Associates, Inc., which was another development company. Under their direction the remainder of this section was bulkheaded, and marshy areas were filled to enable the construction of private homes. At the same time Realty Associates, Inc. built the Bay Park Country Club with its beaches and other recreational facilities as an attractive resort for summer residents of the village.[4]

In 1926, the Bay Park Property Owners' Association was created by residents of the village to provide some of the services that were available in incorporated villages.[5] Despite the efforts of this group, the original goals of the developers were never completely realized. No efforts, however, have been made by the property owners of the area to change the optimistically descriptive designation of this village.

Bayville

The Village of Bayville is composed of two localities which were originally known as Oak Neck and Pine Island. The first reference to the name Oak Neck appears in the Town Records in a deed dated October 24, 1658, by which Daniel Whitehead purchased that area from two Indians named Josias and Rogers. This same deed also contains the first mention of the appellation Pine Island, as being the adjacent property.[1]

On February 4, 1660, Daniel Whitehead transferred ownership of Oak Neck to the people of the Town of Oyster Bay.[2] The Town, in turn, on November 30, 1666, issued an order that: "all ye Medow one Oake Neck & pine Neck shall be forthwith Laid out to ye Inhabitants of ye Towne to Every allotment his Equall Sheare."[3] To ensure their ownership of this land, the Town of Oyster Bay obtained a confirmatory deed in 1711, which stated:

> We arumpus, Werah, Seahor and Surrocan the Indians and Chief Proprietors of ye Metenacock Lands In ye pattent and Township of Oysterbay &c &c For ye sum of Seventy Pounds &c &c do sell &c &c all that one certain parcel of land called and known by ye name of Oak Neck and Pine Island bounded on ye northward side by ye Sound and on ye east end by Hogg Island and on ye southward side by ye saltwater and on ye west end by Mittinecock Line &c &c we are true soles and Lawful owners of ye above bargained premises &c &c.[4]

The names Oak Neck and Pine Island continued to be used until the mid-1800s, at which time the present designation was adopted. An 1859 article stated that: "The name of the area known as Oak Neck will be changed to Bayville."[5] Twenty-one years later a local newspaper gave a more complete description of the adoption of the name Bayville by reporting that:

> A meeting was held at the school house, Bayville, many years ago, for the purpose of considering the subject of changing the name of the place. It was then known as Oak Neck, on account of many old and large oaks which grew in abundance there. After talking over the various names suggested it was finally decided that Bayville would be an appropriate name. This name was adopted because the place is nearly surrounded by water and vessels can come to most any part of it, load and unload their cargoes with safety, and can have plenty of good water in getting on and off the shore except when tides run very low.[6]

Since 1859, therefore, the name Bayville has been used as the designation of this village which was incorporated on May 8, 1919.[7]

Bellerose

The Village of Bellerose is of relatively recent origin when compared with many other villages in Nassau County, but no record has yet been discovered as to why its name was selected. Still several theories have been formulated as to the origin of the name of this area which is located between the villages of Floral Park and Queens Village.

The first of these theories states that a farmer named Joseph Rose, who had owned this property, had devised this designation in honor of his daughter, who was named Belle. This is untrue, as none of his daughters, nor his wife, was named Belle, as can be seen in the census records and his will dated October 15, 1923. His wife was named Theresia, and his daughters were Mary, Theresia, and Bernadine.[1]

Another possibility suggested was that roses were grown there by the many florists and seed suppliers who had their businesses in this area. With the many beds of beautiful roses which may have been growing there, it was felt that someone prefixed the word "Belle," or "beautiful" in French, to the word rose and so the name came into existence.[2] While this theory can neither be proven nor disproven, seed catalogues issued by John Lewis Childs, in the early 1900s, show that he was selling a rose known as the Belle Rose.

Finally, it has been stated that Mrs. Helen M. Marsh, who began developing this section in 1910, was the person who had devised the name Bellerose.[3] This is totally erroneous as it was reported on August 23, 1898, that:

> A party of nearly a score of florists from Manhattan and Brooklyn visited Belle Rose, a small settlement lying between Queens and Floral Park, for the purpose of looking over the land with a view to laying out immense gardens for the growth of flowers and flower seeds. Bell Rose was laid out for building purposes several years ago, but the

property has not found a very ready market, notwithstanding its desirability and convenient and healthful location. The land lies adjacent to the gardens of the Hon. John Lewis Childs, and the success of the latter has impressed others with the adaptability of the soil for flower raising purposes. One of the party said that if satisfactory arrangements could be made in the event of their finding the land all that had been claimed for it, there was a strong probability that a syndicate would buy the land and engage in the seed and flower growing industry. The land is within a short distance of the easterly line of the City of New York, and is certain to prove very valuable before many years have passed.[4]

While that syndicate was never formed, this article does offer a possible explanation for the origin of the name Bellerose. As was stated, "Belle Rose" was laid out several years prior to 1898, for building purposes. This occurred when, on April 29, 1893, Frank Phelan purchased the former Rose property from George J. Bryan and Edward V. Hallock, for $49,000.[5] At that time it was reported that this property would be laid out into building lots and put on the market by the Citizens Real Estate Company of Brooklyn, of which Phelan was an agent.[6] It seems likely, therefore, that this company coined this euphonious name in the hope of attracting prospective settlers, which never occurred because of the financial depression of the 1890s. The Citizens Real Estate Company was undoubtedly responsible for getting the Long Island Rail Road to erect a station named Bellerose for the use of the homeowners they hoped would be living there. This station was located on the south side of the tracks, about one thousand feet west of the present station. It is listed in railroad timetables as early as October 1898.[7]

When Mrs. Marsh began her development in 1910, the old abandoned depot was still standing with a sign showing it had been the Bellerose station. She then adopted the existing name for her village which was later to be incorporated on April 3, 1924.[8]

Bellerose Terrace

The village of Bellerose Terrace is an unincorporated area situated between the Village of Bellerose and the New York City line. Originally it had been composed of two large farms, which today would have been on either side of the Cross Island Parkway.

The land to the west had belonged to Valentine H. Hallock and later was owned by his son, Edward V. Hallock. They were florists and seedmen, and Edward V. Hallock was to become the president of the Society of American Florists.[1] Following his death on March 2, 1909, this land and his home were retained by his estate until the mid-1920s.

The property to the east had been the farm of Henry R. Dunham before being purchased by John Betts in the 1880s. Betts had made a fortune in the brewery business in Pennsylvania and had acquired this farm as a place to spend the warm weather with his family.[2] Following his death in August 1886, his widow,

Elizabeth Betts, made this her primary residence and lived there at least until 1923.[3]

Development of this area in the late 1920s appears to have begun in the eastern section and worked westward. Originally this locality was given the name Bellerose Gardens West, which appears on maps filed in the office of the Nassau County Clerk and on deeds as late as the 1930s. Eventually a fire company was formed and, under the name of the Bellerose Terrace Chemical Engine and Hose Company, Inc., purchased land for a firehouse in 1927.[4]

For a while both the names Bellerose Gardens West and Bellerose Terrace seem to have been used to designate this area. The reason Bellerose Terrace was finally chosen as the sole name is unknown. Possibly it was because, when the streets in the Village of Bellerose were laid out, they were graded at a higher level and separated from Bellerose Terrace by hedges. This may have led the residents to refer to their area as the "terrace," and this became the name which was adopted.

The use of the names Bellerose Terrace and Bellerose Manor and Bellerose Lawns in Queens County were resented by the residents of the incorporated Village of Bellerose. Their civic association claimed in 1939, that theirs was the only community entitled to use Bellerose in its name. Their complaints went unheeded, and this community has retained the name Bellerose Terrace.[5]

Bellmore

On March 28, 1676, the Town Records show that John Smith conveyed his meadow lands at Little Neck to his son, Jeremiah Smith.[1] This is the first known reference to the locality which became the village of Bellmore. The names Little Neck and Little Neck South, to distinguish it from the Little Neck in Queens County, continued to be used until the early 1800s.

In 1818, a new bridge was built over the creek which separates what was then known as Whale Neck from Little Neck, and the name New Bridge was applied to the area bordering both sides of this bridge. Nathaniel S. Prime, while writing of the neighboring village of Merrick in 1845, stated that: "*Newbridge* is a name applied to the eastern part of the same continued settlement, in the south-east corner of the town."[2]

The residents of this village did not feel that it was a part of Merrick, and they called a meeting to consider the propriety of changing the area's name. This meeting was held on December 11, 1858, at the home of William Baldwin. Allen Baldwin was chosen chairman. After defining the boundaries of the village, a resolution was passed requesting that the name of the place be changed, and on the first vote the designation of Bridgehaven was adopted. It was also resolved that this name be put into use immediately and that the proceedings of the meeting be published in the local newspapers.[3]

This meeting might never have been called had the actions of a previous meeting, held on December 1, 1858, at the house of John Jackson, been publicized. At this meeting residents of Little Neck, Newbridge, and Smithville selected Stephen Baldwin to act as chairman. A resolution was passed authorizing the change of the designations of these areas. The names New Bridge and Cedar Valley then were offered, and a majority of the residents voted to adopt Cedar Valley as the new name for the entire area.[4]

Great confusion arose from the actions of these meetings, and those who favored each name refused to accept the other. For this reason, Smithville was retained as the name for the north Bellmore area, and New Bridge continued to be used for the locality to the south. The name New Bridge was still in use when the South Side Rail Road of Long Island built its line through this village in 1869, and constructed a station there in October of that year. In May 1870, the name Bellmore appeared on railroad timetables for the first time, and that designation was used in addition to New Bridge for several years.[5] In 1873, both New Bridge and Bellmore Stations appear on a map showing this village; however, the name New Bridge was abandoned shortly after this, and the village became known simply as Bellmore.[6] Unfortunately, no mention was made as to why the railroad selected the name by which this village has been known since 1870. It should be noted, however, that the apocryphal story of Bellmore receiving its name because a railroad engineer would ring his bell more when he passed his girlfriend's home in that village is completely fictitious and without merit.[7]

Bethpage

The name Bethpage was first used in reference to the locality which is now the village of Old Bethpage. That section was named by Thomas Powell who purchased it in 1695. As with most areas in Nassau County which were settled by Quakers, this locality was given a biblical name. In this case the designation selected was Bethphage, or Bethpage as it later became known. Powell's reason for choosing this name was that the place was between the villages of Jericho and Jerusalem, as the present village of Wantagh was then known. This corresponded to references in the Bible to Bethphage, which supposedly was located between Jericho and Jerusalem.[1]

The designation of Jerusalem was also adopted by the Bethpage area in the early 1800s, and was used until the Long Island Rail Road constructed a line through that section in the 1840s. At that time the name of this village was changed to Jerusalem Station.[2] Eventually it was decided to further change the name of the village because it was often confused with Jerusalem South, which later was to become known as Wantagh. In March 1867, the names of the post office and railroad station were changed to Central Park.[3] It is said that this name was selected because the village was approximately midway between New Hyde Park and Deer Park.[4]

Further confusion ensued because of the similarity of the name Central Park and the park by that name in New York City. For this reason it was suggested that the name be changed in 1890 and 1891, but no action was taken.[5] The village continued to be known as Central Park until 1936. At that time a committee was formed, with William J. Ahern as chairman, to attempt to have the village renamed Bethpage.[6] Their reason for desiring Bethpage as the new designation for their village was that Bethpage State Park had recently been opened, and they felt the name would promote the value of their property. Ahern wrote letters to George LeBoutillier, Vice President of the Long Island Rail Road Company, and Robert Moses, President of the Long Island State Park Commission, to request their approval.[7] Both responded favorably, and first Assistant Postmaster General W. W. Howes wrote, "If the majority of the patrons desire the name of the post office changed they should submit a petition to the department to that effect."[8]

For this reason a petition was circulated by the Central Park Improvement Committee and forwarded to the Post Office Department in August 1936.[9] It approved the request and stated the name of the post office would become Bethpage effective October 1, 1936.[10] This announcement caused considerable annoyance to the residents of the present village of Old Bethpage since their section had always been known as Bethpage. With the change in the name of the Central Park post office, however, Bethpage became the official designation of this area.[11]

Brookville

The entire Brookville area, including the present Villages of Brookville, Old Brookville, and Upper Brookville, was known by the Indians as Sucos or Suco's Wigwam.[1] William Wallace Tooker said of this name that: "Sucos: the site of the village of Brookville was . . . so called from *Suco,* the Indian who occupied the wigwam. His name is an abbreviation of *Suconamon,* from whom the land was purchased in the early days of the township."[2]

In 1663, Captain John Underhill was given a grant of land by the Town of Oyster Bay, and it is reported in the Town Records that, "John Undrell have 10 eakers between Nicklas wright land by the way to hemsteed and the high way." This land was in the Brookville area and was being referred to as Wolverhampton by 1712.[3]

In his biography of Captain John Underhill, Henry C. Shelley stated of the Underhill family in England that, "it was in the southern region of the midland county of Staffordshire, and especially at Wolverhampton and its vicinity, that the most virile and prosperous Underhill family was seated."[4] It appears obvious, therefore, that the name Wolverhampton had been given to this locality by the Underhill family after their ancestral home in England.

By 1768, the name Wolverhampton had been corrupted or shortened to Wolver Hollow and that designation continued to be used until January 15, 1848.[5] It was then reported that:

> At a meeting of the inhabitants of Wolver Hollow, town of Oyster Bay, Queens County, L.I., held at the District School House Jan. 15th, 1848. Mr. Andris Bogart was called to the Chair, and J. B. Luyster chosen Secretary. The object of the meeting being to change the name of the place called Wolver Hollow to some other more appropriate name.
>
> After some preliminary remarks in regard to a suitable name (there being several names presented) it was resolved to ballot for the new

name which was done, and the name Brookville, received the greatest number of votes.

On motion it was unanimously resolved that the name of the place formerly called Wolver Hollow is now changed and that hereafter it be known by the name of Brookville.[6]

Apparently this change was not welcomed by all the residents of that area, as several letters appeared in the newspapers in protest of this move.[7] Despite these protests, the name Brookville was adopted and has remained in use to this day. On December 14, 1931, this village was officially incorporated.

Carle Place

Silas Carle, a New York City drug merchant, purchased the area located immediately to the west of Westbury in the early 1800s.[1] Although he lived in Manhattan at that time, he was familiar with this area, as his father had been a resident of the Town of North Hempstead.[2]

The property he acquired extended from a point north of Jericho Turnpike, south to the Long Island Rail Road tracks, and was bounded on the east by Westbury and on the west by the future village of Mineola. Opposite today's Carle Road, on the north side of Jericho Turnpike, Carle built a house on this land. It was the showplace of the area which became referred to as "the Carle place."[3]

Eventually the definite article was dropped, and the entire area became known as Carle Place. The first reference found using this name appeared in a Long Island Rail Road timetable which went into effect on June 10, 1837.[4] This designation was to be used from that time until 1895, when a real estate development was begun there. The developers renamed the area Mineola Park, taking this appellation from the neighboring village to the west.[5] Despite the fact that this development proved to be a failure, the name Mineola Park was used in referring to this locality until 1915.[6]

In that year, the residents officially re-adopted the name of Carle Place as the designation of their village. The growth of this area, however, was quite slow until the years immediately following World War II. At that time William Levitt purchased most of the acreage which had composed the abortive Mineola Park Development. Levitt constructed a large number of low cost homes, and the population of the area increased more than four hundred percent in five years. This growth led some of the residents to make one final attempt to rename their village. This occurred in 1951, but general indifference by the majority of the residents doomed this movement.[7]

Although Silas Carle died on January 16, 1861, his home still serves as a reminder of the man who left his name to this village.[8] This house remains on its original site and has become a wing of a later, enlarged house that was owned by Clarence Pell.[9]

Cedarhurst

Cedarhurst was one of the many villages included in the large area which was originally known as Near Rockaway. It was not until the South Side Rail Road of Long Island built a branch line to the Rockaways in 1869, that individual villages began to develop in this area. The first reference to this locality having a separate identity occurred in October 1869, when a railroad timetable listed the area under the name of Ocean Point.[1]

In writing of this village, in 1870, a local newspaper stated:

> About one mile west of Woodsburgh, is the next station on the Rockaway Branch Railroad, Ocean Point. The name is, on first view, a misnomer, as you naturally expect to behold the Ocean in its glory, instead of which you are landed amidst a recently cleared up piece of woodland, a negro house a little to the east of the platform upon which you stand (for as yet Ocean Point does not boast of a Depot), and a small house to the north-west adjoining a beautiful broad avenue.

> Notwithstanding its splendid view of Jamaica Bay, its Southern shores studded with the improvements of East New York, Canarsie, and Western Jamaica, you feel disappointed.[2]

In April 1887, it was announced that the Cedarhurst Company, with A. H. Stevens, President; George C. Rand, Vice President; Frank Storrs, Treasurer; S. P. Hinckley, Secretary; and Charles A. Cheever, General Manager; had acquired the Ocean Point area. The Rockaway Hunting Club, now located in Lawrence, had been established there in 1884, and it was stated that the grounds about the club would be improved for all sports, new roads would be opened, and two hundred and twenty-five acres of land would be laid out for housing sites.[3]

Apparently, the Cedarhurst Company then was able to convince the railroad that the name of their station should be changed from Ocean Point to Cedarhurst. This was accomplished on April 1, 1890, and shortly thereafter the local newspapers began referring to the village as Cedarhurst.[4]

On September 16, 1910, the village was officially incorporated under that name, and no known attempts have been made to change its designation.[5]

Centre Island

The area today incorporated under the name of the Village of Centre Island was originally known as Hog Island. In 1639, this neck of land was sold to Matthew Sunderland of Boston, by the Earl of Sterling. Sunderland's title to this land was later repudiated, as the Dutch felt the Earl of Sterling never had the right to sell this property.[1]

The first recorded use of the name Hog Island occurred in a patent dated April 23, 1659, which stated:

> *Petrus Stuyvesant,* Director-General, etc., and the Council testify and declare, that to-day date underwritten, we have given and granted to *Govert Loockermans, Cornelius van Ruyven* and *Jacobus Backer* a piece of land, situate on *Marten Gerritsen's Bay,* in the Indian tongue

Office was then presented to the meeting and read by the Secretary, and on motion a committee of three was appointed to elect a corresponding number of names from the list, which names were to be submitted to the meeting for a final choice. The three names selected were Elmont, Farmer's Valley and Belle Font. A motion to decide the choice by ballot was carried, resulting in 29 votes, 22 for Elmont and 7 for Belle Font. Thereupon the approval of the name Elmont was made unanimous. . . . After the above business had been transacted the petition to the Postmaster General was read by the Secretary and all present affixed their signatures. On motion a vote of thanks was tendered Mrs. T. C. Hendrickson for the suggestion of the name appropriated and the meeting was dissolved amid great enthusiasm and the rendering of three rousing cheers for Elmont.[5]

In August 1882, it was announced that the Post Office Department had approved the petition to establish a post office there to be known as Elmont. This name has been in constant use since that time.[6] Unfortunately, however, no record giving the reason Mrs. Hendrickson suggested the name Elmont has yet been discovered, so the origin of this appellation remains unknown.[7]

Farmingdale

The Village of Farmingdale was originally part of the large tract purchased by Thomas Powell in 1695. Powell selected the name Bethphage, or Bethpage as it later became known, as the designation for this locality. His reason for selecting this name was that it was located between the villages of Jericho and Jerusalem, as was the biblical Bethphage.[1]

This appellation was generally used until settlement of this large area caused various localities to adopt separate names. The first such name, therefore, to be used for the present Village of Farmingdale was Hardscrabble. This rather unusual designation first appeared in the Town Records on February 12, 1814, when the school district boundaries in the Town of Oyster Bay were redesignated. The name Hardscrabble continued to be used in the Town Records until April 30, 1842. The following year, on December 12, 1843, the name Farmingdale first appeared in reference to this village and it has been in constant use since that time.[2]

The adoption of Farmingdale as the designation of the village was due to the efforts of Ambrose George. A land speculator from Buffalo, George acquired property in the Village of Hempstead in the early 1830s, and made his first purchases in Hardscrabble in 1838.[3] Being an enterprising real estate salesman, George realized it would be difficult to promote an area that had such an unattractive name. For this reason he combined the main occupation of that place with the fact that it was located in a fertile dale and coined the descriptive designation Farmingdale, which was readily adopted by the residents of the village.[4]

In writing of Farmingdale in 1845, Nathaniel S. Prime stated,

Farmingdale, (formerly Hard-scrabble,) is about one mile east of Bethpage, and near the line of Huntington. The change of names is

31

doubtless one of the improvements produced on the island, by the construction of the rail road. And it seems a little remarkable that two places of such uncouth appellations as *Hard-scrabble* and *Punk's-hole,* should have been so situated as to become the only two stopping-places of the Boston train, with its hundreds of passengers every day.[5]

In 1904, the Village of Farmingdale was incorporated under this name which had been in use since 1843. The only known attempt to change that designation occurred in May 1936, when a group of residents petitioned to have the village renamed Bethpage. They felt that they had a right to that name since the railroad station there had been known as Bethpage in 1841. Also, they thought it would be advantageous to the prosperity of the village to be identified with the new Bethpage State Park. This movement failed to gain much support, and it also came too late, as Central Park had already applied to the postal authorities for use of the name Bethpage.[6] An area of this section is known as South Farmingdale, but it has no separate legal identity of its own.[7]

Floral Park

Despite the fact that the Long Island Rail Road ran through the area which is today the Village of Floral Park as early as the 1830s, this locality remained lightly populated and unnamed until the Central Railroad of Long Island arrived there in 1872. In June of that year a depot was built on the north side of Jericho Turnpike and west of Little Neck Road, just west of the present Village of Floral Park.[1] This depot or station was named Hinsdale after Elizur B. Hinsdale, secretary and chief counsel of the then consolidated Flushing and North Side Railroad Company, which was to manage the operations of the Central Railroad of Long Island.[2]

The Long Island Rail Road, which had depended on stations to the west and east at Queens Village and New Hyde Park, realized they would lose the residents of this area as passengers. To prevent this, they created a station on their line which was designated the Plainfield Station. The origin of the name Plainfield is uncertain, but it may have been in reference to the road which ran south from this place to Elmont.

With the establishment of these stations, this locality had two names to choose from, and eventually Hinsdale became the name of the village. When an attempt was made to establish a post office there, the residents were informed they would have to change the village name as there was already a Hinsdale post office in upstate New York. For this reason they renamed the village East Hinsdale and the post office there was officially created on July 17, 1877.[3]

On July 15, 1884, the East Hinsdale post office was closed, and a new office established in the John Lewis Childs seed store using the name Floral as its designation. Although the name Floral was highly descriptive of the area, with the tremendous flower beds which had been established there by Childs and other florists, many of the older residents did not favor it. A majority of the persons living in this area then petitioned the authorities, and the East Hinsdale office was reestablished a month later.[4] Childs continued the fight and, by showing that a majority of the mail had been going through his post office, managed to have it opened again in January 1885. Then, in April 1886, it was announced that the name of the East Hinsdale railroad station had also been changed to Floral.[5] The fact that Childs was able to effect this change while Elizur B. Hinsdale was still counsel for the railroad, shows the tremendous influence he must have been able to exert.

The dispute still had not ended for in May 1886, it was reported that,

> There has been a long and bloodless war between the people of East Hinsdale and J. L. Childs & Co. of Floral, as to who should have the Post Office. The Hinsdale people had their Bull Run some time ago, now Mr. Childs has met his Gettysburg. The Post-Master General sent several inspectors to look over the ground, and has now decided to discontinue the office at Floral, as not being needed.
>
> Mr. M. S. Frost has been appointed Post Master at East Hinsdale in place of Mr. E. V. Hallock, resigned, A new office is now in course of erection . . . attached to the store of W. H. Baylis, to accommodate the increased mails.[6]

Again, John Lewis Childs managed to have this decision reversed, for in June 1887, it was reported that,

> For the third time a post office has been established at Floral, half a mile east of East Hinsdale. The contiquity of the offices led to a good deal of trouble and surprise is expressed at the re-establishment of the one at Floral. . . . It is expected that the East Hinsdale office will be discontinued.[7]

This proved to be the last time the post office was moved, and on May 26, 1887, its name was changed to Floral Park.[8] It was under this designation that the village was incorporated on October 15, 1908, and no further attempts to rename it have been made.[9]

Flower Hill

Like all villages on the Manhasset peninsula, Flower Hill was originally referred to as a part of Cow Neck. When separate communities eventually began to develop on this neck, this area adopted the name Flower Hill. The first use of that designation in the Town Records appeared in a deed dated May 1, 1759, in which Andries Onderdonck transferred land at that place to his brother Henderick Onderdonck.[1]

When the English occupied Long Island during the Revolutionary War, an order relating to the signals to be used on sighting enemy vessels was issued by Major General William Tryon. This order stated, "Signals by day and night for Long Island and Kingsbridge are to be made from Norwich Hill, Sutton's Hill and Flushing Heights. . . . Norwich Hill is two miles south of Oysterbay, Sutton's Hill is three miles from Cow Neck Point, Flushing Heights are near Ustick's house." In a footnote to this order, Henry Onderdonk, Jr., stated that Sutton's Hill was then on the farm of Joseph O. Hegeman.[2] This farm was said by Henry

A. Stoutenburgh to have been located at Flower Hill, therefore, a portion of Flower Hill was known as Sutton's Hill during the Revolutionary War.[3]

In 1860, Flower Hill was referred to in a gazetteer as a "farming neighborhood near the center of Manhasset Neck."[4] This name continued to be used, but with the growth of Port Washington, it was generally considered to be a part of that village. In 1930, rumors began to circulate that Port Washington was about to be incorporated as a city and the residents of Flower Hill decided it would be wise to incorporate their locality to maintain its independence.

Two applications to hold a hearing on the issue of incorporating Flower Hill as a village were rejected on the ground that it would separate Port Washington's school and water districts. Finally, in April 1931, their application was approved and April 27, 1931, was set as the date for the election to determine if Flower Hill were to become an incorporated village.[5]

This election was held in the real estate office of Charles W. Munson, and the residents of the area voted unanimously to become an incorporated village.[6] Incorporation of this village under the name of Flower Hill, by which it had been known since the 1750s, became a reality on May 25, 1931. Unfortunately, no record has been discovered giving the origin of this probably descriptive designation.

Franklin Square

Although this area was at first merely a part of the town common lands on the Hempstead Plains, it began to assume an individual character by the late 1700s. By this time pens had been erected in this locality and the sheep owned by the town's residents were driven there and separated each October.[1] Possibly it was from the activities of this annual sheep parting that this area received its first name, Trimming Square.[2]

This designation was used from the early 1800s until July 1851, when the name of the then emerging village located there was changed to Washington Square.[3] This appellation may have been adopted because the village was near the Washington Course where races and the yearly Huckleberry Frolics took place.[4] Although it is uncertain whether the name was taken from the race track, it obviously was adopted in honor of George Washington.

The name Washington Square was used by the residents of this locality until they attempted to obtain a post office in the early 1870s. Although they received permission to establish a branch office in their village, the postal authorities refused to allow them to use the name Washington Square. The reason was that the Post Office Department felt there were too many places in the state already using the name Washington.[5]

At this time, therefore, the name of the village was changed to Franklin Square, probably in honor of Benjamin Franklin. While there is no documentation that this designation was given to honor Franklin, it seems likely as the residents were replacing another patriotic name, Washington Square.

There appear to have been no further attempts to change the designation of this village since the name Franklin Square was adopted. In February 1929, an attempt was made to incorporate this village. This movement ended in April of that year, however, when Supervisor Robert G. Anderson denied the petition as it had not shown that a sufficient number of property owners had consented to this change.[6]

Freeport

The Village of Freeport appears first to have been referred to variously as Washburn's Neck and Raynor's Neck. The earliest use of the name Washburn's Neck is found in the Town Records in a document dated 1659, and this name continued to be used until the 1700s. It is interesting to note that this same document which relates to taxable property also is the first mention of the designation Raynor's Neck.[1]

These names continued in use until 1725, when the entire area became generally known as South Woods or Great South Woods.[2] Despite the fact that this was the most common designation for that locality, the use of the name Raynor's Neck was never completely abandoned. This was because Edward Raynor had been one of the first settlers there, and his family eventually became the most populous in that area.

Because of the Raynors association with this locality, it began to be referred to as Raynortown or Raynor Town by the early 1800s. In 1845, Nathaniel S. Prime mentioned this growing village as Raynor South or Raynortown.[3] This name was used until 1853, when a series of meetings were held to consider the advisability of changing the designation of the community.

On August 6, 1853, the first of these meetings was held with Willet Charlick, chairman, and A. L. Foote, secretary. On the question of whether to retain the name Raynor Town or adopt the new designation of Bayside Village, Raynor Town won by a vote of seventeen to eleven.[4] The proposed name of Bayside Village was obviously a reference to this village's geographical location, as it is situated on a bay.

This vote did not satisfy the baymen, who were quite numerous, and another meeting was held on August 13, 1853. At this time the name Freeport was offered as a substitute for Raynor Town. This name had a descriptive quality because the harbor of this village was not a port of entry and duties were not collected there. Moreover, Jones Inlet provided easy access, which made the village a truly free port. At this second meeting Raynor Town received thirty votes to a total of twenty-three votes for Freeport.[5]

Again, those who desired a change of name for the village refused to accept defeat, and a third meeting was held on the evening of August 22, 1853, at the home of Benjamin Smith. Elbert Cox was elected chairman and A. L. Foote again served as secretary of what proved to be the final meeting regarding this matter. It was stated that the object of the meeting was to give a permanent name to the village, and the following resolution was adopted, "Resolved, unanimously, that this village be hereafter known by the name of FREEPORT, and not by those of Raynor Town, Raynor South, and South Hempstead, as heretofore."[6] It was under the name of Freeport, therefore, that Freeport received its first post office in 1853, and was incorporated on October 22, 1892.[7]

Garden City

Prior to its purchase by Alexander T. Stewart in 1869, the present-day Village of Garden City was considered to be merely a part of the Hempstead Plains. When Stewart purchased more than seven thousand acres of these common lands from the Town of Hempstead it was announced that he intended to establish a model village there.[1]

In writing of the naming of this village, village historian Vincent F. Seyfried stated,

> At the time of the Stewart purchase, no name had been chosen for the new city envisioned by its founder. In the last months of 1869, people began referring to it as the "City of the Plains" for want of a better title. In January 1870, the newspapers began to speculate as to just what Stewart would name his new city. Some suggested "Alexandria" as a tribute to the founder, and with associations harking back to classical antiquity. Others offered "Stewart City" as an appropriate description of the locality. In February 1870, Stewart revealed his own choice—"Garden City." Surprisingly, the name comes from the city of Chicago! Though persons would search in vain for any resemblance today, the fact is that the Chicago that existed before Mrs. O'Leary's cow kicked over the fatal lantern that wiped out the city in 1871 had been known informally as the Garden City, because of the large and beautiful gardens that graced the private homes of the wealthy. Stewart liked the euphonious sound of the name and adopted it for his own foundation.[2]

According to Seyfried, the earliest written use of the name Garden City that he was able to find appeared in the February 15, 1871 issue of the *Brooklyn Times*. At that time the name was so new that it appeared in quotation marks.

In his history of Long Island, William S. Pelletreau wrote of Stewart's attempt to establish this village that,

> He conceived the idea of erecting a town which would in its way be a model community, a little republic, a revival in nineteenth century days of the old theocratic settlements. It would be far enough away from New York to keep away excursion parties, its land should be common property and should not be sold outright, and even the houses would be built by the corporation and only leased to the settlers. It would be a complete community within itself; it would make and enact its own laws, have a large hotel capable of accommodating the most refined travelers, wide streets, superb schools, and all manner of modern improvements and equipments. Everything would be hedged about with restrictions, the place would be exclusive and refined, and the entire community should be so commend itself that it would be regarded as a garden spot—a veritable Eden. . . .
>
> So the place received the name of Garden City.[3]

To ensure the fact that this descriptive designation would become a reality, Stewart purchased thousands of trees and shrubs from Prince's Nursery in Flushing and had them planted on the previously barren plains land.[4] Among them were many rare trees imported from Europe, and they may still be seen surrounding some of the older remaining houses.

Unfortunately, Stewart died in 1876, before his village could become a reality.[5] His heirs, however, carried out his plans and although they eventually sold the property, it truly became a garden city and was incorporated under that name in May 1919. Several sections of this village have acquired their own designations, such as Garden City East and Garden City Estates, but they are merely portions of the incorporated Village of Garden City. Also, a locality to the south of this village was given the name Garden City South. However, this is merely an unincorporated part of the Town of Hempstead and has no individual identity.[6]

Garden City Park

During the Revolutionary War, the Queens County Courthouse in Jamaica was destroyed by the British troops quartered there. For this reason a new courthouse was eventually constructed in 1786, and the site selected was a part of what is now the village of Garden City Park.[1] Before Queens County was separated, this locality was the geographical center of the county which was the reason for its selection.

After this courthouse was built the small village which grew about it assumed the names Queens Court House and North Hempstead, after the town in which it was located. A gazetteer published in 1813, stated, "The Village called Queens Court-House, or North-Hempstead . . . hardly deserves a local name or notice but that the Courts are held there."[2]

The name North Hempstead persisted at least until 1836, for in that year another gazetteer was published which mentioned it, stating that in addition to the courthouse, "there are here also, 2 stores and 2 taverns, and a small collection of houses."[3] The following year, however, a local newspaper contained a letter which mentioned an apparent change in the name of the village. This letter stated,

> Mr. Editor;—Sir, I understand by the rumors in circulation that the is-to-be ville at the depot, or stopping place of the L.I. Railroad, near the Court House, is to be christened Clowesville; in compliment no doubt to Mr. Timothy Clowes, the fortunate proprietor of the locality. And though I would not pluck a feather from the plume of Mr. Clowes, I would respectfully suggest from its proximity to Queens Court House, and central position, the propriety of naming it Queensville.
>
> And unless Mr. Clowes, already extensively known as a Teacher and leader of youth through the Academic groves of science, is also ambitious to have his name go down to posterity on the spire of a villa, I think he can have no reasonable objection to so appropriate and euphonous and appellation for this, his favorite location.[4]

Despite this appeal, the name Clowesville was adopted, and it continued to be used until 1873. A map bearing that date in the Nassau County Clerk's Office refers to this area as Hitchcock's Garden City Park.[5] Being an enterprising real estate developer, Benjamin W. Hitchcock attempted to benefit from the publicity being given to Alexander T. Stewart's growing village of Garden City. For this reason he borrowed that village's descriptive name and added "Park" to it.

Hitchcock subdivided this tract into 646 building lots in the summer of 1874, and constructed a depot which was known as Garden City or Garden City Park.[6] Although this name caused much confusion for travelers and was resented by the residents of the Village of Garden City, Hitchcock refused to allow this appellation to be changed. The name Garden City Park has been in continuous use since it was adopted in 1873, and no known attempts to change it further have been made.

Glen Cove

In 1668, Joseph Carpenter, Nathaniel Coles, Robert Coles, Daniel Coles, and Nicholas Simpkins received a patent for the area that was to become the City of Glen Cove.[1] This area was known by the Matinecock Indians variously as Mosquetah, Musceata, Muskitoe, Musketo, and Musketa. William Wallace Tooker states: "This name appears modernly as 'Mosquito Cove,' and has the appearance of being derived from that irrepressible insect, but it was not. It takes its name from the extensive meadows bordering the cove or creek. Variations are *Mosquetah,* 1658; *Musceata,* 1667; *Muskitoe,* 1668; *Muchito,* 1675. *Mosquetah* corresponds to Narragansett *muskkosqut,* 'meadow'; Mohegan *mux-quataug,* 'place of rushes.'"[2]

This designation was adopted by the settlers, who added the descriptive word "Cove" to the name.[3] Eventually it was corrupted, through constant usage, until the place became known as Mosquito Cove. According to George W. Cocks, who spoke on local place-names and their derivations at the Glen Cove Library Lyceum in 1897, this gradual change was, "The inevitable tendency . . . towards a familiar sound notwithstanding the prejudicial effect of its use on the reputation of the place as a residence."[4]

The first post office in the village of Musquito Cove was established on December 18, 1818. On November 6, 1833, the name of this post office was changed to Moscheto Cove, in an apparent attempt to disassociate the area with the thought of the annoying insect.[5] This attempt at camouflaging their name through a new method of spelling was not successful, and finally a meeting of the residents of the area was held to solve the problem.

At this meeting at the house of Joshua T. Wright on February 4, 1834, it was decided that the existing name was preventing further settlement in the area, as well as harming business, and must be changed.[6] Among the names suggested for consideration as the new designation for the village were Regina, Circassia, and Pembroke. As far back as 1773, the village had been called Pembroke by many of the inhabitants, but this name was never legally adopted.[7] None of these names, however, was favorably received by those present at the meeting, and eventually the name Glencoe was suggested, after a place in Scotland. According to Henry J. Scudder, who recorded this event in 1868, "Some person present, misunderstanding the name, and thinking the speaker had said Glen Cove, exclaimed, 'That's it! That's the name—we can still say going up to the Cove.'"[8] This name was unanimously adopted, but unfortunately there is no record of who suggested Glencoe or who misinterpreted it as Glen Cove.

Prior to 1918, Glen Cove was an unincorporated village and part of the Town of Oyster Bay. In 1917, an application to become the first city in Nassau County was made to the State of New York. According to the City Clerk, upon receiving approval a special referendum was held, a charter adopted, and Glen Cove officially became a city on January 1, 1918.[9]

Glen Head

The area which now comprises the village of Glen Head was originally known as Cedar Swamp. This name first appears in the Town Records in a deed from David Underhill to James Townsend, dated November 17, 1697, and continued to be used at least until October 25, 1865.[1] The designation of Cedar Swamp seems to have been descriptive, as the area was thickly overgrown with cedar trees.

Although the name Cedar Swamp was still being used as late as 1865, a meeting of the residents of that place had been held in July 1855, and they voted to adopt Glenburn as its new designation.[2] Why that name did not come into general usage is unknown. Frostville was still another name used by a section of the Cedar Swamp area in the 1860s.

Prior to the Civil War, the Long Island Rail Road Company had planned a branch line to run to Glen Cove.[3] This line did not become a reality until December 1864, when it was reported that the railroad had reached Frostville. The next month the first mention of the name Glen Head appeared in an article which stated,

> It has seemed impossible to fix upon a name for the terminus of the Branch Road, until an inflammatory looking bill appeared styling it "Glen Head," and signed "A. Reasoner." Now, if ever there was a reasonable conclusion it is no mortal reason for giving it this awful, barbarous sounding name. The prefix "Glen" is too common already—it is attached to cove, lake, creek, street, hall, house, valley, mont, and mount, and now (abominable) head. But the new is suggestive of a more appropriate and better one than any yet stated, Pumpkin Head—Pumpkin Head Depot. It is capital—just the thing.[4]

This article mentioned several other humorous suggestions received by the newspaper, such as Red Head and Swell Head, as possible names. In all probability, however, the railroad had coined the name Glen Head because this was the railhead of the line to Glen Cove.

Although the railroad had designated its station Glen Head, the local post office retained Cedar Swamp as its name until June 1866, when it was changed to Greenvale.[5] Later it was again changed to Glenwood and finally in January

1874, to Glen Head, the name of the railroad station, This designation has prevailed.[6] It is interesting to note, however, that the names Greenvale and Glenwood were later adopted by other villages in this area.

Glenwood Landing

On July 5, 1681, Isaac Doughty purchased from the Indians the area that was to eventually become the village of Glenwood Landing. The first name for this area was Newark, sometimes also referred to as Newwark and New Work.[1] This designation is believed to have come from Doughty's place of birth in England and first appears in the Town Records in a deed confirming Doughty's purchase dated March 6, 1684. Newark continued to be used as the name of this area until 1753, at which time it last appeared in the Town Records. After this date, the locality was generally known as Littleworth, which was actually the designation of the future Village of Sea Cliff.[2]

Glenwood first appears as a place-name in the Town Records in 1864, but at that time it was being applied to the locality which became Glen Head.[3] When the area around the present Glen Head railroad station relinquished the name Glenwood, it gradually was adopted by the community situated on Hempstead Harbor and was in use by 1873.[4] As was the case in the development of the name Glen Head, Glenwood or Glenwood Landing received its name because of its proximity to Glen Cove. Therefore, it can also claim to evolve indirectly from Glencoe in Scotland.

In January 1892, it was announced that the community's application for a post office had been accepted. To avoid confusion with villages having similar names, however, it was necessary to change the designation of this place. Because there was a steamboat landing located there, the word "Landing" was added to the existing name of Glenwood. In March 1892, the post office opened as Glenwood Landing and this has been the official designation of the village since that time.[5]

Great Neck

The Village of Great Neck takes its name from the peninsula of the same name. This neck of land, however, had previously been known as Madnans Neck. That designation first appeared in the Town Records in a deed dated January 8, 1668.[1] It has been suggested by Benjamin F. Thompson, and other historians, that Madnans was an Indian name.[2] The fact that this appellation does not appear until 1668, however, would tend to dispute this theory, for the name would almost certainly have been used at an earlier date.

William Wallace Tooker does not offer any opinion as to the origin of this designation, but states that Madnans or *Madnank:* "may be abbreviated from a longer name, for it seems to contain the inseparable generic *adene,* 'hill,' and *auke,* 'land,' or 'place,' signifying therefore some kind of a 'hilly place.'" As the Matinecock Indians would have provided this designation, if it were of aboriginal origin, it would seem most appropriate for the name of their own area can be translated as being descriptive of high land.[3]

Because the north shore of Long Island from the eastern section of Queens County to Western Suffolk County contains numerous necks of land or peninsulas, the settlers eventually began to give them more descriptive designations. For this reason the two western peninsulas became known as Little Neck and Great Neck. The first recorded use of the appellation Great Neck, in place of Madnans Neck, appeared in the Town Records in a deed to Robert Jackson dated March 8, 1672.[4]

As was the case of adjoining Manhasset Neck, the entire area of this peninsula was known as Great Neck. Eventually, however, separate communities began to become established and they adopted their own names. Today the appellation of Great Neck is retained only by the villages of that name. No known attempts have been made to change the designation of the present-day Village of Great Neck which was officially incorporated in 1922.[5] An area known as Great Neck Gardens, although geographically separated from the Village of Great Neck, is merely an unincorporated portion of the Town of North Hempstead with no official identity of its own.

Great Neck Estates

All of the Great Neck peninsula was originally known as Madnans Neck. That designation first appeared in the Town Records in a deed dated January 8, 1668.[1] The name Madnans Neck was eventually replaced by that of Great Neck, and the first record of this designation appears in the Town Records in a deed to Robert Jackson dated March 8, 1672.[2]

Great Neck continued to be used as the designation for most of this area until the early 1900s, when separate communities began to evolve. The area which formed the southwest corner of this peninsula, however, continued to use the descriptive designation of Great Neck. This section differed from the other localities in this area in that it had been purchased from the Indians by Richard Thorne in the 1600s, and remained in the possession of his family until the turn of the twentieth century.[3] For this reason no extensive development took place there until new residents began to arrive in the early 1900s.

These residents decided to incorporate their village so they would be able to maintain home rule and also to obtain services which were not available from the Town of North Hempstead. The name Great Neck Estates was selected at the time this village was incorporated in 1911, and it has been in continuous use ever since.[4]

Great Neck Plaza

The incorporated Village of Great Neck Plaza was originally a part of that large area which was known simply as Great Neck, after the peninsula that designation describes. This locality began to assume a separate identity when the North Shore Rail Road Company built a branch line to it in 1866, and created a station there. This station was originally known as Great Neck, but in November 1869, its name was changed to Brookdale. That designation was used until May 1872, when it reverted to Great Neck.[1]

The entire area which is now the Village of Great Neck Plaza became the property of William R. Grace, later Mayor of New York City, in a most unusual manner. It has been reported that,

> W. R. Grace was a rail passenger one day, and that he had to use the washroom en route. Unfortunately, the washroom on the train was locked, which caused the future Mayor of New York considerable discomfort and embarrassment, and for which he successfully sued the railroad for $2,400. But the railroad happened to be broke even then and, in settlement, gave him all of what is now Great Neck Plaza, which he later subdivided.[2]

Grace, who had married Lillian Gilchrist in 1859, named his newly acquired property Thomaston, in honor of his wife's ancestral home in Maine.[3] The name Thomaston, however, never became popular with the residents of this area and eventually it was abandoned. Later that designation was adopted by a locality to the southeast of Great Neck which is now known as the Village of Thomaston.

The railroad proved to be the dominant feature of this locality, and a village began to grow there. Because of the plaza surrounding the railroad station, this area was referred to as "The Plaza" by the residents of this village. When it was decided to incorporate the area in May 1930, the citizens' committee which was instrumental in this movement, decided to add that name, which was already in popular use, to the former designation of Great Neck.[4]

Greenvale

The first use of the name Greenvale was in reference to the present-day village of Glen Head. That locality's original name was Cedar Swamp, and its use can be dated as early as November 17, 1697.[1] In July 1866, the name of the post office there was changed from Cedar Swamp to Greenvale. Shortly thereafter it was again changed to Glen Head, which the railroad had named the station located there, and that name has prevailed.[2]

During this period, the area which is now the present village of Greenvale was referred to as being north of Hempstead Harbor and later as north of Roslyn or North Roslyn. When the railroad constructed its branch line through this section, a depot was erected there which was known as Week's Station by 1866.[3] That designation continued to be used until a new station was built there in June 1897, and named Wheatly Hills.[4]

This name was not acceptable to all the residents of this area, and in a letter in the *East Norwich Enterprise,* Halstead H. Frost stated,

> Wheatly Hills is the name of a new R. R. Station near Roslyn. Wheatly Hills are three or more miles distant from the location of the station. There can be no intelligent reason given for such a name in this location. So soon as we learned that there was to be a new station near the Roslyn cemetery we suggested the name of "Bryant's Rest"

as the immortal poet rests tranquilly in his honored tomb, which is marked by a substantial monument, not one hundred yards from the new station. The name we give is, most surely, an appropriate one, and as beautiful as appropriate. We beg of the intelligent, wealthy men of Wheatly Hills to change the name forthwith and show their appreciation of one of the sweetest poets of his time, and a man who was in all practical affairs of life as nearly perfect as men can well be.[5]

Although Frost's suggestion was not adopted, the name Wheatly Hills did not long remain in existence for, by the early 1900s, this locality had been renamed Greenvale.[6] The name Greenvale, however, was not the only designation for this region as the main crossroads became known as Bull's Head. That appellation had been taken from the Bull's Head Hotel, located on the northeast corner of Northern Boulevard and Glen Cove Road, which was noted for its large sign with a picture of a bull's head.[7]

The name Bull's Head, in addition to Greenvale, continued to be used at least until 1914, after which the latter designation alone was retained.[8] Possibly the name Greenvale was meant to be descriptive of the area or euphonious, but its origin remains unknown.

Hempstead

Hempstead, the first village settled in Nassau County, has had a great deal of controversy over the origin of its name, which came into existence in 1643. Two views have been offered by well-qualified historians, but the place of origin of this name remains unproven at this time.

The first theory is that the name was derived from the birthplace of John Carman, one of the original patentees. Carman was born at Hemel-Hempstead, Hertfordshire, England, and his fellow purchaser, Rev. Robert Fordham, was born only eighteen miles from that place.[1] Therefore, it is concluded that the founders of the settlement named the place after an English town which was very familiar to them. This theory is endorsed by Benjamin F. Thompson, in the first edition of his *History of Long Island*; Benjamin D. Hicks, editor of the *Records of the Towns of North and South Hempstead*; Bernice Schultz, author of *Colonial Hempstead*; and George D. A. Combes, former historian of the Town of Hempstead.[2]

The second theory states that the area when settled was under the control of the Dutch and was named for Heemstede, "the neatest little village on the Island of Schowen in Zeeland."[3] The supporters of this view are John Romeyn Brodhead and Dr. Edmund Bailey O'Callaghan, who collaborated in presenting that monumental series *Documents Relative to the Colonial History of the State of New York*.[4]

Combes offered probably the most logical answer to the problem. He reviewed all the available evidence and concluded that the name Hempstead was of English origin. He proved that of the six original patentees (John Strickland, Rev. Robert Fordham, John Ogden, John Carman, John Lawrence, and Jonas Wood), three came from Hertfordshire. The Hertfordshire men were Carman,

Fordham, and Lawrence. Carman actually came from the town of Hemel-Hempstead. Combes also cited as further evidence to his English origin theory the old English meaning of Hempstead, "Hem" or "Ham," a "town," and "stead," a "locality, place or spot."[5] This translation of the name corresponds to frequent early references to Hempstead in the Town Records, as the "town spot."[6]

On July 25, 1853, Hempstead became the first incorporated village in Nassau County.[7] No known attempts have been made to change the name of this village. However, a local newspaper once stated that, "We like the name of Hempstead. It is an old, substantial, well-worn, and time-honored appellation, but we live in a day of new things, and we throw out the suggestion, whether it would not be well, *when* we apply for an act of *city incorporation,* to style ourselves the *City of the Plains.*"[8]

Hempstead Gardens, East Hempstead, and South Hempstead are localities which have taken their names from the Village of Hempstead. None of these areas are actual incorporated villages or have any officially recognized existence.[9]

Herricks

The name Herricks is primarily used today in referring to the present Union Free School District No. 9. Originally created in 1813, as district No. 10, it became Union Free School District No. 9 in 1818.[1] This school district is bounded on the north by Roslyn, on the east and south by Mineola, on the west by New Hyde Park, and on the northwest by Manhasset. Although this was one of the earliest settled localities in Nassau County, it has become an unincorporated area of the Town of North Hempstead, and has almost been absorbed by its neighboring villages. This may be observed by the fact that the residents of Herricks are served by five distinct post offices—Albertson, Manhasset, New Hyde Park, Roslyn, and Williston Park.

The first recorded use of the name Herricks appears in the Town Records when an acre of land there was granted to Symon Seren on March 24, 1659.[2] This designation was taken from the Herricks family members who were among the first settlers in the Town of Southampton. A census of that town, taken in 1698, shows that James Herricks was then residing in the village of Bridgehampton. It was James Herricks' brother, William Herricks, who settled in this section of Nassau County and who gave his name to the area.[3] This appellation has been in constant use since it was first adopted in the 1650s, and there have been no known attempts to change the name of the locality.

Hewlett

Despite the fact that the name George Hewlett's Point appears as a place-name in the Town Records as early as July 2, 1718, the use of Hewlett as a village name did not occur until 1869.[1] Prior to that date, this village was part of that large area which was known as Near Rockaway. When the South Side Rail Road of Long Island began the construction of a branch line to the Rockaway area, however, many localities along this line received individual names.[2]

The section that was to become the village of Hewlett first appeared on the timetables of the railroad in June 1869, as Cedar Grove. This name did not remain in existence long, however, for in October of the same year, the station was renamed Hewletts.[3] The designation of this station and the village was changed because Samuel M. Hewlett had deeded land to the railroad for the station with the stipulation that it be known as Hewlett to perpetuate his family name.[4]

After the South Side Rail Road of Long Island became a part of the Long Island Rail Road in 1876, a number of station names, including Hewlett, were eventually altered.[5] These changes were made because Long Island Rail Road President Austin Corbin did not wish to perpetuate the use of what he considered to be proprietary place-names. For this reason the name of the Hewlett station was changed to Fenhurst in 1890.[6]

The village of Hewlett, however, had established its post office in 1889, and the area's residents refused to rename it Fenhurst. Therefore, the village was to have the postal name of Hewlett, while the railroad station was known as Fenhurst. By 1893, this confusing situation caused the residents to send a petition to the Long Island Rail Road Company requesting that the station again be renamed Hewlett.[7] No action was taken on this request, despite the fact that the Hewlett family had donated the land for the station with the stipulation that it always be known as Hewlett or the land would revert to the family.

In February 1897, another petition was sent to the railroad stating that, "The name Fenhurst is a misnomer as the place is not a boggy wood nor a grove." The railroad, however, again declined to act on the petition, and the name Fenhurst remained in use until June of that year. At that time the Long Island Rail Road Company announced a change of their former policy by stating that the names of all railroad stations must be the same as that of the post office.[8]

Possibly the death of Austin Corbin, in 1896, was the reason for this change of policy on the part of the Long Island Rail Road Company.[9] Another reason may have been the fact that Augustus J. Hewlett gave the railroad an additional strip of land, thirty-one feet wide, running from the station to the Trinity church-yard. This gift was based on the condition that: "The station shall be for ever named and known as Hewlett."[10] This name, therefore, has prevailed to this day with no further attempts to change it.[11]

Hewlett Bay Park

The first mention of the name Hewlett Bay Park was not in reference to the village of that name, but was the designation of a steeplechase course. This exclusive track owed its existence to Carleton Macy, a prominent resident of the area, who conceived the idea of laying out this beautiful course. Its name was taken partially from the nearby village of Hewlett, because it was near Woodmere Bay, and because of its park-like appearance.[1]

During the 1920s, this area began to be developed primarily by Joseph S. Auerbach, senior member of the law firm of Davies, Auerbach, Cornell, and

Hardy. According to John P. Duncombe, former Village Clerk of Hewlett Bay Park, it was Joseph S. Auerbach who was responsible for the area officially adopting the name although maps show it was in use as early as 1914.[2]

The village was officially incorporated on September 20, 1928, and a local newspaper stated, "The primary reason for incorporation . . . lies in the fact that they want to preserve the exclusiveness of the development and feel that this can be done only through incorporating and adopting their own zoning ordinance and building code." Hewlett Bay Park, therefore, became the twentieth village in the Town of Hempstead to incorporate, and it was one of the smallest, comprising only 38/100 of a square mile.[3]

Hewlett Harbor

The Village of Hewlett Harbor received its name because it was situated on the water, had a harbor, and was near the Hewlett railroad station.[1] According to former Mayor George Auslander, this village, like Hewlett Bay Park, was developed by Joseph S. Auerbach who had a large estate there. It was Auerbach who suggested the name, for the above mentioned reasons, and it was adopted by the area's residents.[2]

This village was primarily developed during the 1920s, and a petition was sent to the Presiding Supervisor of the Town of Hempstead requesting permission to incorporate. This petition was accepted and, after the residents of the area voted favorably, Hewlett Harbor became an incorporated village on October 7, 1925.[3] Since the time Joseph S. Auerbach suggested the name, there have been no attempts to change the designation of this village.

Hewlett Neck

The Village of Hewlett Neck was the last to be named of the three areas which took their designations from the village of Hewlett. In 1927, the name Hewlett Neck was suggested by William S. Pettit, a lawyer and local historian, who was one of the leaders in the movement to incorporate the village.[1]

Pettit decided upon this appellation because of this section's historic connection with the Hewlett family members who were the earliest to settle here, because the place was near the village of Hewlett, and because it was on a neck of land adjoining Woodmere Bay.[2] This name was acceptable to the area's residents and was used when they petitioned the Town of Hempstead in January 1927, for permission to incorporate.[3] The village was officially incorporated under the name of Hewlett Neck on March 30, 1927, and that designation has been in continuous use since that time.[4]

Hicksville

On May 20, 1648, Robert Williams purchased from Pugnipan, sachem of the Matinecock Indians, the area that today includes Hicksville, Woodbury, part of Jericho, Plainview, and Bethpage.[1] Williams retained possession of this land until his death in 1681, after which it began to be divided among a number of families who played important roles in the history of the Town of Oyster Bay.[2] Despite this division, the area continued to be known as the Williams Plantation until the individual localities there assumed separate identities and adopted their own names.

The first known use of the name Hicksville appears on a map of that area which was surveyed for the Hicksville Association in October 1836. They proposed to develop this area, and the name Hicksville was selected to honor Valentine Hicks, who founded the Association with Robert and David Seaman.[3] The reason for the use of his name, in addition to his being one of the founders of the Association, was that he was then President of the Long Island Rail Road Company and had arranged to have the railroad line run through their property. The railroad contributed greatly to the development of the village when the financial panic of 1837 halted work on the line, and Hicksville became its terminus for a period of four years.[4]

Despite Valentine Hicks' close connection with the founding and development of this village, an erroneous theory came into existence that it had been named to honor his uncle, the famed Quaker, Elias Hicks.[5] This theory was perpetuated by a number of historians, and not until the 1940s was Valentine Hicks recognized as the true founder of this village.[6]

The name Hicksville has been in constant use since it was first adopted; however, there have been several attempts to change the designation of the village. The first of these attempts occurred in 1893, when it was announced that a movement had begun to change the name of Hicksville to Waldorf, in honor of William Waldorf Astor.[7] The leader of this movement was John J. Pollock, a summer resident of Hicksville, who had acquired large land holdings there. His reason for desiring this change of name was that he felt Astor would build a new depot for the village and assist it financially for the honor it had bestowed upon him.[8] This proposal was rejected by the residents of the village that year and again in 1895 and 1896, at which time Pollock finally abandoned the idea and adopted the name Waldorf Park for his own property.[9]

In 1921, the businessmen and some of the residents of the village were reported as tired of being referred to as "hicks from Hicksville." One of the village's leading citizens, Judge Joseph Steinert, however, mustered enough supporters to end any attempt at changing the designation of the village.[10]

A final attempt to rename the village occurred in 1926, and Manetto, Lincoln, Merryville, and Washington were suggested as possible substitutes. Although both the Chamber of Commerce and the Civic League were in favor of changing the name, the residents of the village decided to retain the designation of Hicksville by a vote of 944 to 317.[11] Since that time no further attempt has been made to abandon the name under which this village was founded in 1836.[12]

Inwood

The present-day village of Inwood was the first locality in the area originally known as Near Rockaway to receive its own designation. The Town Records show that a town meeting was held on January 16, 1663, and state:

> There was given and granted to Mr. Robert Ashman, Thomas Hickes, John Ellison, Thomas Ellison, Hope Washburne and Abraham Smith, the whole point of upland at Rockaway, Commonly Called by the name of the Northwest Point for them and their successors to Inioy [enjoy] for ever.[1]

The name Northwest Point, or North West Point, remained in use until 1871. At that time a local newspaper reported that: "Westville is the new name for that part of Rockaway formerly known as 'North-West Point.' Its fine locality, increasing population and growing wealth and importance would all seem to combine to make it worthy of the more euphonious and aristocratic title—Westville." It was also announced in this article that the next movement to be made by the residents of the village would be to establish a school so the children would not be forced to attend the one located east of the post office at Lawrence.[2]

Because of the fact that this village did not have a post office, a meeting was held in the Reading Room Hall on December 29, 1888, to consider the questions of changing the name of the village and establishing a post office. At this meeting it was announced that the population of the village was more than eleven hundred persons and that it contained twenty-two business establishments.[3] When it was decided that a post office would benefit the village in many ways, it became necessary to select a new name as Westville was already being used by a post office in upstate New York. The meeting was called to order by J. D. Crosby; counselor A. Mutch was chosen chairman. A motion was made and carried that the name receiving the highest number of votes would be adopted. Among the names suggested were Radwayton, Inwood, Bayhead, Custer, Pike's Peak, Springhaven, Raway, and Elco. The name Inwood was adopted. It had been suggested by William L. Kavanagh, apparently because the old name North West Point reminded him that the northwest point of Manhattan Island was also known as Inwood.[4]

With the adoption of this new designation, it was possible for the village to establish a post office, which was opened on February 25, 1889, with J. D. Crosby as postmaster.[5] This post office was used until about 1920, when it went out of existence, probably because the volume of mail passing through that office did not justify its being retained. In 1932, it was reported that the application to establish a new post office in that village was being studied and, if approved, mail would no longer have to go through the Far Rockaway post office as it had for the past twelve years. It also was announced at this time that if the application were approved, the name of the village undoubtedly would have to be changed to prevent confusion with the Inwood section of New York.[6] This application was eventually denied, and Inwood did not receive a new post office until 1949.[7]

At that time there were no objections to the name of the village, so it was allowed to remain unchanged.[8]

Island Park

Hog Island was the original name of the Village of Island Park. The first reference to that designation appeared in the Town Records in a deed dated June 21, 1665, from Thomas Ireland to Mearck Mages.[1] The name Hog Island continued to be used from that time until 1874, when the entire island was offered for sale.[2]

At that time the Board of Supervisors was considering the purchase of the island as a new site for the county poor farm. The Supervisors, however, hesitated in making this purchase, and a syndicate of New York City men entered negotiations to acquire the island as a resort and hotel site. At this point Mrs. Sarah A. Barnum, the wife of Peter C. Barnum, a noted New York clothier, took action and purchased the property before the syndicate could complete their negotiations.[3]

Mrs. Barnum, who was a noted philanthropist, had taken an interest in bettering the conditions of the county's paupers, and called the Supervisors' attention to this island as a perfect site for the poor farm. After learning that the New York syndicate proposed to acquire the island, she drove eight miles through a snowstorm the night before the deal was to be completed and purchased it in her own name.[4] Mrs. Barnum then offered the island to the county at the same price she had paid.

The *Southside Observer* reported that the Board of Supervisors had passed a resolution which stated: "Resolved, That if Hog Island be purchased by the county for a county poor farm, that the name of the island be changed, and That Mrs. P. C. Barnum be requested to select a name for said island." The same issue of this newspaper announced that the Supervisors had purchased the island from Mrs. Barnum. However, they did not give her a chance to rename it as they changed its designation to Barnum Island.[5] In reply to the *Long Island Farmer,* the *Observer* stated: "The 'Farmer' wants to know by what authority the name of Hog Island was changed. As that journal is not very well posted on county affairs we would inform it that the name was changed by authority of a resolution passed by the Board of Supervisors on May 21, 1874."[6] The often-told story of Barnum Island being named for P. T. Barnum, who supposedly had acquired that area as a place to winter quarter his circus, is totally erroneous. P. T. Barnum never had any association with this locality, but possibly the similarity of his name and Mrs. P. C. Barnum led to the creation of this spurious legend.[7]

When the Long Island Rail Road built a branch line to Long Beach in 1880, it ran across Barnum Island and stations were established there.[8] The principal station was known as Barnum Island; however, a secondary station was located at the south end of the island and named Wreck Lead. That designation was changed briefly to Queens Water in 1900, but shortly reverted to its former name.[9]

The following year the name of the entire island was changed to Jekyl Island, which is also the designation of an island off the Georgia coast, and it was reported that:

> The syndicate who purchased recently the old Barnum Island poor house farm from Nassau County, at $40,000 was composed principally of leading Tammany Hall politicians, who have changed its name to Jekyl Island, would contract at once to have a one mile race track built, grand stands erected, etc., with large club house building, spending at least $200,000 in improvements. The track will be ready for the next Spring meetings.[10]

This ambitious project was never realized, and the area remained largely undeveloped until the early 1920s, when it was acquired by the Island Park-Long Beach Corporation. Under the leadership of L. M. Austin, Jr., and C. N. Talbot, this area began to be developed. At the same time the island was given the descriptive name of Island Park, because it was completely surrounded by water and they visualized its park-like appearance.[11] In November 1926, the Village was officially incorporated as Island Park when 107 out of 114 votes were cast in favor of the proposition.[12]

Island Trees

The name Island Trees has all but gone out of existence, as most of its former territory has been absorbed by what is now known as Levittown. Island Trees, as a designation, first appeared in the Town Records in a deed dated March 22, 1747, but it seems to have been in use for a number of years prior to that date.[1] Through the years, variations of the name Island Trees were Island of Trees, Isle of Trees, and Isle of Pines.[2] This designation was descriptive of the area, as it referred to a small group of trees located on the otherwise almost treeless Hempstead Plains. It was described in 1804, by Timothy Dwight, President of Yale College, as follows:

> We entered Hempstead plain, and dined at a place called the Isle of Pines, situated near its centre. . . .

> Hempstead plain is, I presume, the easternmost of those "American prairies which are too fertile to produce forest trees"; unless it should be thought that the little cluster of pines, amid which we dined, vitiates its title to this extraordinary character. . . . The Isle of Pines, at a distance, resembles not a little a real island.[3]

The name Island Trees continued to be used until 1948, when the appellation of Levittown was adopted by most of the area which had previously been known by the more descriptive and historic designation. In 1947, Abraham Levitt and Sons had purchased large tracts of what was then primarily farmland and constructed the village which was to bear their name.

When the appellation Levittown was adopted in 1948, there was a great deal of dissent on the part of both the new and old residents of the locality. The name Levittown prevailed, however, and Island Trees has been relegated to a small area which consists mainly of a school and water district.

Jericho

The area which became the village of Jericho was originally part of the land purchased from the Indians by Robert Williams in 1648.[1] During the 1600s, this area, as well as most of the Town of Oyster Bay, was designated simply as Oysterbay (one word). Gradually the names of Jericho, Lusum, The Farms, and Springfield, came into use when referring to the section that became the village of Jericho.[2] These names were often used simultaneously during the period from about 1660 to 1690, but eventually all were joined under the common name of Jericho.[3]

Lusum was said by historian Benjamin F. Thompson to be an Indian name.[4] William Wallace Tooker, however, stated that, "The name is probably not Indian, but a contraction from the name of a village in England called *Lewisham*, now a part of London."[5] In speaking before the Glen Cove Library Lyceum in 1897, George W. Cocks agreed with this statement by asserting, "This name has been claimed as an Indian name, but I prefer to believe that it is English and a recollection of *Lewesham*, formerly a suburb of London. The east part of Lusum was some time known as Springfield and the western as 'the Farms,' but finally Jericho was adopted, including the three."[6]

The name Springfield came from the Jericho Spring Pond which existed until 1958, when it was destroyed by the building of a cloverleaf for the Long Island Expressway.[7] No record exists, however, as to the origin of the name The Farms. It has been suggested that this designation simply referred to a number of farms which were located in that area.

Jericho appears to have been a name that was given to this area by Robert Williams. The first known use of this designation appeared in the Town Records when Williams sold property on the plains at Jericho to Robert Forman in 1662.[8] This name is a typical example of the biblical place-names which were used by the Quakers.

Gradually the use of the other names for this area subsided and, by 1694, Jericho had become the designation of the settlement that was to be established there.[9] The first post office opened in the village of Jericho in December 1818, and there have been no known attempts to change the name of this village.[10]

Kensington

Kensington, like all villages on the Great Neck peninsula, was originally referred to as part of Madnans Neck. This name, which was believed to be of Indian origin, first appears in the Town Records in a deed dated January 8, 1668.[1] William Wallace Tooker, however, stated that: "The early forms *Madnans* or *Mad-Nans* . . . suggest that the name is not of Indian origin, but may have been so-called from some crazy squaw or white woman. Again, *Madnank* may be abbreviated from a longer name, for it seems to contain the inseparable generic *adene*, 'hill,' and *auke*, 'land,' or 'place,' signifying therefore some kind of a 'hilly place.'"[2]

By 1672, the name Great Neck had replaced Madnans Neck as the designation of the peninsula.[3] The future Village of Kensington, therefore, was generally referred to as Great Neck until it was developed as a separate entity. This development began when Charles E. Finlay and Edward J. Rickert purchased the old Allen farm, later the Deering farm, in 1909.[4] Because this was an era of great real estate expansion on Long Island, the various developers vied with each other to attract purchasers.

The Ricket-Finlay Realty Company then decided that their development must be a model village. Their attention, therefore, was brought to the beautiful village of Kensington in England, with its world-famed gardens. For this reason they selected that name for their development. They erected gates on Middle Neck Road which were designed to duplicate the famous gates at the entrance to England's Kensington Gardens. In November 1917, this 135 acre tract became an incorporated village under the appropriate name its developers had selected.[5]

King's Point

Like all villages on the Great Neck peninsula, the area which is today the Village of King's Point was originally known as a part of Mad Nans Neck and then as Great Neck. In 1756, Joseph Hewlett purchased the northern part of this peninsula from Luke Haviland, and it became known as Hewlett's Point. When Joseph Hewlett died, this property was left to his son, Lawrence Hewlett, who in turn bequeathed it to his son, Joseph Lawrence Hewlett.[1]

Joseph Lawrence Hewlett was the last member of that family to own the entire estate. After his death in 1849, his children began selling portions of their holdings on the peninsula.[2] One of the purchasers of land there was John Alsop King, son of former Governor of New York John Alsop King, and grandson of the famed Rufus King.[3] After acquiring this land in 1854, John Alsop King began developing this northern section of the peninsula. He erected an elaborate mansion and lived there until his death on November 21, 1900.[4]

As early as March 24, 1868, this area was being referred to as King's Point in the Town Records.[5] This name has prevailed to the present day. However, the previous designation of Hewlett's Point has been preserved by the northernmost tip of land on this peninsula.

In 1924, the residents of this locality decided that it would be advantageous to become an incorporated village.[6] At that time, in addition to the village known as King's Point, there were also the small villages of East Shore and Elm Point. These three sections merged and, in November 1924, were officially incorporated as the Village of King's Point.[7]

Lake Success

The Village of Lake Success takes its descriptive designation from the body of water which bears that name. This lake, which is located near the center of the village, was originally known as Sacut, a name which had been given to it by the Matinecock Indians. According to William Wallace Tooker, Sacut signifies: "'at the outlet,' the components being *sac* (= *sauk*) 'an outlet of a pond,' 'a stream flowing out of a pond or lake'; and the locative affix - *ut,* 'at,' 'near,' 'by,' etc. *Saco* in Maine is another form of the word. The Long Island *Sacut* is the equivalent of the Delaware . . . *sakuwit,* 'mouth of a creek, mouth of a river.'"[1] Benjamin F. Thompson stated of the name Sacut that, "by a simple deflection in sound it might have been and probably was changed to Success."[2] Tooker agrees with this theory as being the most probable reason for the adoption of this appellation.

The name Success first appeared in the Town Records, in reference to the lake and general locality, in a deed dated September 22, 1679, which describes land owned by Richard Cornell.[3] The designation Success Pond, or simply Success, was used from that date until the 1800s.

In 1835, however, the residents of the area decided to change the name of their locality and Lakeville, again in deference to the nearby lake, was adopted.[4] Ten years later, in writing of this area, Nathaniel S. Prime stated, "*Lakeville* is a name applied to the vicinage of Success Pond, though there is no settlement here that deserves the name of a village."[5] Although the designation Lakeville was to be used for almost the next hundred years, it has almost ceased to exist. Today this name is only perpetuated by Lakeville Road, which is the primary road running in a north-south direction through the village.

When the residents of the area decided to incorporate their village on December 9, 1926, they voted to re-adopt the former name of the village. For this reason the old name of Success came back into existence as a result of the proximity of the lake. In December of the following year, however, the residents of the community decided to rename it the Village of Lake Success. No further attempts to change this name have been made.[6]

Lakeview

The village of Lakeview was a lightly-settled area located between Hempstead and Near Rockaway, which in Revolutionary times was referred to as the Hempstead Swamp.[1] By the 1860s, two communities named Schodack and Woodfield had begun to develop in this area.

There appears to be some evidence that the name Schodack was of Indian origin. As early as 1865, there was a town in Rensselaer County where the villages of Schodack Depot and Schodack Landing were located.[2] In writing of this name, Dr. Albert B. Corey, New York State Historian, stated,

> I happen to be interested in this name because I live in the Town of Schodack in Rensselaer County, in fact within one mile of Schodack Center which you would have difficulty in finding if you drove through it.
>
> The name Schodack means "the fire place of the council fire." It is commonly regarded as the traditional Mahican capital which was on the site of the present Castle-on-Hudson.[3]

The name Woodfield came into existence on February 14, 1863, when a meeting was held at the home of Stephen Langdon for the purpose of choosing a name for "the place on the road from William Rhodes' to Joseph B. Langdons." At this meeting it was resolved that "this place be hereafter known as, and called Woodfield."[4]

In 1870, the South Side Rail Road of Long Island began to construct a branch line which ran through this area. From Valley Stream this line crossed Malverne and a station was established there. A second station was built in what was to be the village of Lakeview, where the line crossed Woodfield Avenue. It was named Woodfield depot.[5]

That name continued to be used until 1903, when it was reported,

> Lake View, although it is not yet on the map, is the name of a railroad station on the Hempstead and Valley Stream branch of the Long Island Railroad, north of Woodfield. It is a picturesque place and well worthy of a visit.

> A map of the Woodfield Road, from Hempstead avenue, West Hempstead, to Lake View avenue, Rockville Centre, has been made. We understand the road is to be made 50 feet wide and otherwise improved. . . . The new railroad station here is a benefit to the property and residents of this section, and it is patronized by many passengers.[6]

By 1905, it was noted that the name Lake View had definitely succeeded Woodfield.[7] This appellation was spelled as two words until 1926, when it was changed to the present spelling to avoid conflict with the name of an upstate community.[8] The reason this descriptive name had been devised by the railroad was because the area overlooked the lake which the Brooklyn Water Supply Company had created as a reservoir in the 1870s.

Lattingtown

The Latting family (also spelled Lattin, Latten, Latin, and Latine), was one of the earliest to settle in the Town of Oyster Bay.[1] Their name first appears in the Town Records on September 25, 1660, when Richard Latting purchased land in the locality that was later to bear his name, from Ann Croker. This deed indicates that Latting had formerly been a resident of Huntington before moving to present-day Nassau County.[2]

This family prospered and by the early 1700s, owned much of the land in the area of the present-day Village of Lattingtown.[3] The first recorded use of that appellation as a place-name occurred in the Town Records in a deed dated January 23, 1742. This deed referred to the locality as Latten Towne, but by the 1750s it had assumed its present form.[4]

According to the village historian, the name came into common usage because of the number and importance of the members of the Latting family.[5] Unfortunately, no records seem to exist as to which member of the family gave his name to the area, or who was responsible for suggesting the designation.

When the residents of the locality decided to incorporate in October 1931, there seems to have been no question but that Lattingtown should be the official name of their village.[6] There have been no known attempts to change the designation of this place since the name was first adopted.

Laurel Hollow

Originally the area which includes the Village of Laurel Hollow and a portion of Cold Spring Harbor was known by the Indians as Wauwepex. William Wallace Tooker stated that, "The name *Wauwepex* represents *Waure-paug-es-it,* 'at the good little water place or pond.' The locality took its name from some 'good spring of water' as did probably the English name of 'Cold Spring.'"[1]

The English settlers, however, selected the more descriptive designation of Laurel Hollow due to the fact that laurel trees grew in abundance in this locality. That name first appeared in the Town Records in a deed dated April 6, 1700, granting land to Thomas Youngs.[2]

The name Laurel Hollow remained in use until the early 1870s and was the source for the designation of a resort hotel that was constructed there.[3] This hotel, known as Laurelton Hall, was built by Dr. Oliver Livingston Jones on a part of his family estate on the west side of Cold Spring Harbor. This three-story hotel was managed by experienced hotel men and proved extremely popular. A long wooden pier was built a short distance from this hotel and boats of the Iron Steamship Company arrived there daily from New York City.[4]

Undoubtedly the excursionists and boarders going to this hotel referred to the area simply as Laurelton, after the hotel, and by 1873, this had become the name of the village.[5] Until 1935, the name Laurelton was in constant use, but in that year a movement was begun to change the designation of this village, which had officially been incorporated on July 27, 1926. The reason the residents of this area wanted the name changed was because a great deal of confusion was being caused for the postal authorities, due to the fact that there was another village known as Laurelton in Queens County.[6] Although that village was of much later origin, having been developed by the Laurelton Land Company in 1905, it had a much larger population and almost all the mails were being delivered there.

For this reason it was reported that,

> A proposition authorizing a change in the village's name from Laurelton to Cold Spring Cove will be submitted to voters of that tiny municipality at the annual village election June 18 it was announced today.
>
> Supporters of the movement for the change claim residents have no objection to Laurelton as a name but simply because this monicker causes considerable confusion, due to the fact that there is another community by the same name on Long Island. . . . The new name, Cold Spring Cove, was selected by the local village board whose members said it was favored from a list of names because it was euphonious and territorially appropriate. The proposition reads simply, "Shall the name of this village be changed from Laurelton to Cold Spring Cove?"[7]

The name Cold Spring Cove was never adopted, however, because the Post Office Department felt its similarity to Cold Spring Harbor would create new confusion. For this reason the residents of the village decided to re-adopt the old designation of their locality, and the name of the village was officially changed from Laurelton to Laurel Hollow on December 20, 1935.[8]

Lawrence

Until the South Side Rail Road of Long Island built a branch line into that section in 1869, the future Village of Lawrence was generally referred to as a part of Near Rockaway.[1] The railroad, however, opened the area to development, and among those attracted to this locality were Newbold Lawrence and his brothers Alfred N. and George N. Lawrence.[2]

The Lawrence brothers, who were originally real estate speculators in New York City, purchased all the farms in this neighborhood and began to lay out their property as an exclusive residential village. Their original plan was to establish a high-class summer resort for New York businessmen. As a part of this plan, they erected a railroad station at their village which was donated to the railroad.[3] They named this depot Lawrence Station, and no one had the temerity to suggest any other name for the village. Therefore, when the Lawrence station was opened in June 1869, this became the name of the village.[4] In July 1886, however, consideration was given to changing its name from Lawrence or Lawrence Station to Lawrence by the Sea. This had been suggested because there were already two other Lawrences in New York State. Apparently nothing came of this proposal, as the name of the village remained unchanged.[5]

Daniel D. Lord, James R. Keene, Foxhall P. Keene, and Russell Sage were among the influential persons to settle there. To maintain the exclusive qualities of this locality, they decided to incorporate the village. This occurred on July 16, 1897. Before the newly-incorporated village was even one year old, however, it almost lost its separate identity. This happened in 1898 when, under the Greater New York City charter, the village of Inwood and most of the Village of Lawrence were included in the city's fifth ward. Assemblyman Wilbur G. Doughty, however, persuaded the legislature to pass a bill which restored these areas to the Town of Hempstead.[6] There have been no attempts to change the name of this village since the designation of Lawrence first came into existence in 1869.[7]

Lawrence Beach

The history of the area which was to become the village of Lawrence Beach was identical to that of the Village of Lawrence until 1884. At that time, Rufus W. Leavitt purchased the section located immediately south of the present Village of Lawrence from the Lawrence family and began its development.[1]

Leavitt named his property the Isle of Wight after that famous English resort, and erected a large hotel there in 1885. This hotel, named the Isle of Wight Hotel, was immensely successful until it was destroyed by fire ten years later. Leavitt also attempted to develop the remainder of the section by dividing his property into building plots and held an auction for the sale of this land in October 1889.

This sale, however, proved unsuccessful, and eventually the area passed into the possession of G. Howard Leavitt.[2]

In the mid-1890s, G. Howard Leavitt sold this land to a syndicate known as the Lawrence Cedarhurst Company and at this time the name Lawrence Beach came into existence.[3] The reason for choosing this name was that the village was bordered by the Village of Lawrence on the north and by the Atlantic Ocean on the south. This name has been in continuous use since that time.

Levittown

Levittown, which replaced the much older name Island Trees, is the most recent of all Nassau County place-names, as it came into existence in 1948. The designation Island Trees was first used in the Town Records in a deed dated March 22, 1747, but it seems to have been in use for a number of years prior to that date.[1] Variations of the name Island Trees were Island of Trees, Isle of Trees, and Isle of Pines. This name was descriptive of the area, as it referred to a small group of trees located on the otherwise almost treeless Hempstead Plains. It was described in 1804, by Timothy Dwight, President of Yale College, as follows,

> We entered Hempstead plain, and dined at a place called the Isle of Pines, situated near its centre. . . .
>
> Hempstead plain is, I presume, the easternmost of those "American prairies which are too fertile to produce forest trees;" unless it should be thought that the little cluster of pines, amid which we dined, vitiates its title to this extraordinary character. . . . The Isle of Pines, at a distance, resembles not a little a real island.[2]

Until the end of World War II, Island Trees remained a largely undeveloped farming community. Early in 1947, however, William Levitt announced plans to create a large housing development in that area. Within less than a year he won the Hempstead Town Board's permission to build cellarless houses with radiant heat, and began his development, which was to win national attention.[3]

The first three hundred families moved into rented houses on October 1, 1947, and by that date, eighteen homes were being completed each day.[4] Shortly after this, Levitt announced his plan to change the name of the development to Levittown, in his honor. This created some controversy and one person wrote to the local newspaper as follows:

> There hasn't been a smiling face on the block (and not many in this whole community) since our name has been changed from Island Trees to Levittown. Although Mr. Levitt insisted on the change, and the name appears on his new signs, the tenants seem to ignore it and continue (and will continue) to call the place Island Trees, and have their mail deliveries, etc., addressed that way.
>
> Eventually, Mr. Levitt hopes to sell these houses—and many of his present tenants will be his prospective buyers. And how many of them will want to buy in a place called Levittown. None!

If Mr. Levitt's name had been Schmollenhoffer or McGilli-
cuddy—or such—would he affix the name "town" to either, and expect
three cheers from the tenants?[5]

Although there was a certain amount of discontent, as expressed by the writer of this letter, Levitt, as principal landowner, did manage to have the name of the village changed to Levittown. Since that time there have been no serious attempts to change it and the use of Island Trees has been limited to the designation of a school district.[6]

Locust Valley

Chechagon, or Chechagon Swamp as it is first referred to in the Town Records in a deed dated January 2, 1681, was the original name for the Locust Valley area.[1] William Wallace Tooker stated that this appellation was the name of an Indian chief who was mentioned in a deed in 1683.[2] This designation was generally used until the early 1700s, when a mill or factory was built in what became known as the Old Kaintuck Mill section of this area.[3]

According to Halstead H. Frost, this mill produced a flaxen material known as buckram, which was used in the manufacture of clothing. Frost stated that,

> The fabric then manufactured in the quaint old mill was well-
> known, and highly valued, and at that time was an attractive class of
> "dress goods," and its name, "Buckram," was a familiar one to all the
> country roundabout, and in this way the locality became known as
> Buckram.[4]

The first reference to the name Buckram appeared in the Town Records, when George Frost was chosen as overseer of highways for Buckram on April 7, 1741.[5] This designation was used until 1857, when the residents requested that the name of their village be changed to Locust Valley.[6] The reasons they wished this change to be made were that the old designation of Buckram was felt to be detrimental, and that the name Locust Valley would be more descriptive of the area. The latter was undoubtedly true, for in the early 1700s, Captain John Sands had brought locust trees to this section of Long Island, and they had multiplied rapidly.

John A. Searing, who had been elected to Congress in 1856, was instrumental in having the name of the village changed to Locust Valley.[7] In December 1857, a local newspaper reported,

> Among the first of the official acts of the Hon. John A. Searing,
> we take pleasure in recording, that through his influence, at Washing-
> ton, the name of Buckram has been changed to Locust Valley. Here-
> after the latter will be the post-office address. We congratulate the
> inhabitants that the name Buckram is now obsolete.[8]

Despite the fact that the names Buckram and then Locust Valley had been in constant use since the 1740s, they were not accepted by all the residents of this locality. When the Quakers had built a meeting house nearby in 1725, they designated it the Matinecock Meeting House. Throughout this entire period, according to Halstead H. Frost, the Quakers living in this locality always headed their letters Matinecock, which they felt was the most appropriate name for the settlement.[9]

In 1902, the Quakers almost received their desire, for it was reported that, "A concerted effort is being made to have the United States postal authorities change the name of this place to Matinecock. Several prominent people, among whom is said to be President Baldwin of the L.I.R.R. who has a summer residence here, are back of the movement."[10] Although it was felt at that time that the designation of the village would be changed, no further action was taken, and Locust Valley was retained as the village name.

Long Beach

The first reference to Long Beach occurred on Christmas Day in 1678, when the Town Council of Hempstead granted property there to forty-two of the Town's freeholders.[1] At this time the area was known as Long Neck or Long Neck Beach, and that designation continued to be used in the Town Records until as late as the year 1722.[2] After that date this locality became known simply as Long Beach, which is a particularly descriptive name for this island which runs some seven miles along the south shore of Nassau County.

In 1725, fifty-nine descendants of the original forty-two freeholders met and deeded the property to Jacob Hicks. After Hicks' death, the ownership of Long Beach passed to the Lawrence family, Carman Frost, and Richard Sandivoord. Eventually a large portion of it became the property of the Town of Hempstead after a lawsuit which ran from 1898 to 1902.[3]

During this entire period, the name of this locality was Long Beach. In 1893, however, it appears that an attempt was made to change the designation of this island. A local newspaper reported that, "The proposed change in the name of Long Beach to 'White' Beach does not meet with the approval of our people. There are, however, so many 'Long Beaches' that a change of name would seem to be desirable."[4] Despite the fact that it may have appeared desirable to some to change the name of Long Beach, this attempt was defeated, and no further attempts were made to change its appellation.

During the early 1900s, extensive development and settlement occurred at Long Beach under the leadership and guidance of ex-State Senator William H. Reynolds. By 1912, the area had become sufficiently populated to consider incorporating the village. The first step in this direction occurred when a meeting was called on May 13, 1912. This meeting followed a refusal on the part of nearby Oceanside's residents to grant Long Beach a school. After first approving this move, they had taken away an appropriation which would have made possible the building of a school, and also refused to increase their school board to give Long Beach a member.[5] Shortly after this, the residents of Long Beach voted to officially incorporate their village under that name.

The incorporated Village of Long Beach did not remain in existence long, as the area became a city on April 22, 1922. This occurred when the charter of the new city was approved by an act of the Legislature entitled Chapter 635 of the Laws of 1922, and it officially adopted the name by which it had been known since 1678.[6]

Mention should also be made of Lido Beach which, while not truly a village, is a settlement located between Point Lookout and Long Beach. Envisioned by ex-State Senator William H. Reynolds, it was intended to become a resort that would be comparable to the Lido in Italy, from which its name was taken. Today, this locality is primarily the site of a county and town beach and golf course, and is served by the Long Beach post office, school district, and sewer district.

Lynbrook

Most sources state that the Village of Lynbrook had been named Bloomfield by 1785, but this seems to be in error. On February 1, 1853, it was reported that a "portion of Hempstead, Queens County, Long Island, within a mile and a quarter of Wood's Corner, has been named Bloomfield."[1] This appears to have been the earliest use of that name for a portion of this area. By the 1850s, the name of the village had been changed to Pearsall's Corners, in honor of the Pearsall family which owned a great amount of land in that area. There are two theories as to the member of the Pearsall family after which the village was named. The leading candidates for this honor are Wright Pearsall, one of the early settlers, and Henry Pearsall, who operated a store in the village.[2] The name was slightly altered in 1870, when the citizens voted to call it Pearsallville. The name was shortened to Pearsall's in 1873, when the first post office was established there.[3]

In 1891, a local newspaper announced that some of the village's residents were in favor of changing its name. Some of the names suggested were: Corbin, in honor of Austin Corbin, President of the Long Island Rail Road; Bristol, after the ship which had been wrecked on the beach opposite that place; and Roanoke, supposedly after the Indian name for wampum, which was made in the vicinity.[4] None of these appellations, was adopted.

In 1892, Bristol, Austin, Roanoke, Newington, Centerville, Marietta, Sandringham, Sparta, Galilee, Damascus, Ceylon, Memphis, Plymouth, and Prospect Plains, were mentioned as possible substitutes for Pearsall's. One resident felt that any of these names would be preferable to the existing designation and stated, "Have we any more reason for naming our village Pearsalls than for calling it after Necubhadnezzar or Phil McCool?"[5] His feelings, however, were not shared by the majority of the residents, and the name Pearsall's again remained unchanged.

In 1893, only the names Wyndermere and Lynbrook were suggested, and a poll was taken by the Improvement Association in August of that year. This poll showed that the residents of the village were almost unanimously in favor of adopting Lynbrook as the new name for the village. The Long Island Rail Road Company approved of the new name and agreed to change the designation of its station when the government changed the name of the post office. After a slight delay the postal authorities also approved the change, and it went into effect on May 1, 1894.[6]

The name Lynbrook was suggested by Thomas P. Brennan, the local agent of the railroad in that village. He devised it by reversing the syllables of Brooklyn, and thereby obtained Lynbrook.[7] The village was officially incorporated on March 15, 1911, and there have been no attempts to further change this name since it was adopted in 1894.[8]

Malverne

The present-day Village of Malverne was for many years a part of that large area which was generally known as Near Rockaway. In 1870, however, the South Side Railroad of Long Island constructed a branch line from Valley Stream to Hempstead. Stations were then created along this route to serve the residents of the various areas through which this line passed. One of these stations was located where the track crossed Hempstead Avenue, near Cornwell Avenue, and it was named Norwood Station or simply Norwood.[1] It is said that this name was suggested by William L. Wood, who ran a general store on the east side of Hempstead Avenue.[2]

The railroad was indirectly responsible for another name which was applied to this area, but it was a derisive appellation that was never officially used. This name, Skunk's Misery, came into existence because of a railroad siding that was built near Franklin Avenue for the firm of Gene and Wright. This company's sole business was supplying manure to farmers who drove there from miles around. It is said that when the wind was coming from the direction of this railroad siding, the atmosphere was so malodorous that people wondered how even skunks could endure it.[3]

The official name of Norwood, however, was still in existence when the Amsterdam Development and Sales Company purchased a number of farms in 1911, and began to develop the area.[4] By this time, however, there were three other villages in New York State which were also known as Norwood. This created a great deal of confusion and inconvenience due to mail being sent to wrong places. It also caused an inability to establish a post office in this area, as a village in St. Lawrence County had already received the name of Norwood for its post office.[5]

Finally action was taken in acquiring a distinctive name for the village when a water pump sent to Ernest Child was delivered to St. Lawrence County by mistake. As Mr. Child was an official of the Eimer and Amend Company, the financial backers of the Amsterdam Development and Sales Company, a meeting was held to settle the matter of choosing a new name. The names suggested at this meeting were Coniston, Hardis, Lynmouth, and Malvern. Malvern was proposed by Ernest Child, who was evidently impressed by the beauty of England's Malvern. The majority of the people in attendance at the meeting, however, were in favor of Lynmouth as the new name for their village.[6] Alfred H. Wagg, manager of the development company, then went to the Long Island Rail Road Company to request that the name of their station be changed to Lynmouth. This name was rejected by the railroad on the basis that it was too similar to Lynbrook and would cause further confusion. When asked for an alternative name, Mr. Wagg remembered Ernest Child's glowing description of Malvern, England, and requested that name. This was acceptable to the railroad, but they inadvertently added the letter "e" to the name, which appeared in their timetables as Malverne. Since February 14, 1918, therefore, this village has been known as Malverne; as such it received a post office in 1919, and officially became an incorporated village on April 4, 1921.[7]

Manhasset

The entire area from Manhasset north to Sands Point was originally known to the settlers as Cow Neck. This name first appears in the Town Records in an agreement dated April 23, 1669, relating to a fence which had been built across the base of this peninsula.[1] It was so named because with the addition of this fence, it became a natural pasturage and common grazing land for the cattle owned by the residents of the town.

The settlement, which grew at the site of present-day Manhasset, adopted its name from the peninsula or neck of land and was known as Head of Cow Neck. This name, or simply Cow Neck, was used until the 1830s, at which time it was deemed unsuitable by the area's residents. A meeting was therefore held at the inn of Allen and Hayden, on January 26, 1837. At this meeting a resolution was passed stating, "that measures should be taken without delay for the selection of some suitable name for the place now called 'Cow Neck,'—some name which shall be unconnected with any disagreeable, mean or unpleasant associations, and which will be likely to meet the approbation of the great body of this community." A further resolution called for the appointment of a committee of twenty prominent residents to make a study of the names they felt were suitable. They were then to report back on February 25, 1837, to present the name that the majority had agreed upon.[2]

The names considered by this committee were: Plandome, which was the name of the home of Singleton Mitchell; Millport, because several mills were in the vicinity; Locust Branch, on account of the locust groves which covered the area; Robinia, the botanical name of the locust tree; and Branch Bay, because the peninsula had a peculiar branching shape. The committee reported at a public meeting held at the house of Israel H. Baxter on February 25, 1837. They stated that the majority of their body was in favor of the name Robinia. This name was, therefore, accepted and resolutions were passed that notice of this change be given to the local newspapers, and that captains of steamboats running to that place be requested to use the name Robinia rather than Cow Neck, Head of Cow Neck, or Cow Bay. A further resolution was passed that, "the thanks of the meeting be presented to Washington Irving, William R. Prince, and Grant Thorburn" for their sentiments in favor of the name Robinia.[3]

The use of this name was to be very short, for by March 8, 1837, it was reported that Robinia was not the true botanical name of the locust tree, but that it was the genus Hymencea.[4] As the name was no longer appropriate, Robinia was dropped, and use of the old name of Cow Neck was continued.

Another meeting was held in June 1837, and the name Manhasset was adopted by the committee which had been formed to make the selection. The reasons for their choice are unknown, but it may be possible that they believed the name Manhasset had been associated with that area. One contemporary newspaper stated, "This, we understand, was the ancient Indian appellation of the Neck."[5] Another reported that it was "a name at once euphonious and aboriginal—the Manhasset Indians having once erected their wigwam at that place."[6] Any knowledgeable student of Long Island history would realize, however, that Manhasset or Manhansett was the Indian name for Shelter Island in Suffolk County and the name Europeans used for the Indians who lived there. Algonquianist William Wallace Tooker gives the meaning of this name as "an island sheltered by islands."[7]

Therefore, possibly through an error, this village has been known by a particularly inappropriate Long Island Indian name since 1837. The section known as Manhasset Valley was given that name in October 1843. Previously it had been called the "Head of Great Neck."[8]

Manorhaven

The history of the Village of Manorhaven was identical to that of its neighboring village of Port Washington until the 1850s. This locality was then known as Dodge's Island because it had been owned by the Dodge family and was almost completely surrounded by water.[1] By 1873, this property had become known as Sunny Side. Shortly thereafter, it was acquired by Richard O'Gorman and its name was changed to O'Gorman's Island. It continued to be owned by Richard O'Gorman and his family from the 1850s until the 1890s.[2]

In February 1894, a local newspaper reported that "John H. Starin has secured control of O'Gorman's Island, at Port Washington according to the *Brooklyn Times,* and will open a summer resort there similar in many respects to Glen Island [across Long Island Sound, south of New Rochelle]. In addition to his excursion steamers he has given out his intention to run a big steamer each day between New York and Port Washington for the passenger and freight traffic."[3]

Apparently Starin's plan to promote O'Gorman's Island into an elaborate summer resort failed, and eventually the property was sold to Jacob Cocks.[4] After Cocks' death this land was sought after for many years by a number of real estate development companies, but none of them was successful. In May 1926, however, it was announced that Jacob Cocks' heirs had sold this property to a syndicate headed by Major B. S. Black of Great Neck. This syndicate, which appointed G. A. Blasser as sales agent, announced that the name of O'Gorman's Island had been changed, and thereafter it would be known as Manhasset Isle.[5]

It was proposed to enlarge the existing seventy-five acres of this property by adding another forty acres of filled-in land.[6] The island was connected to the mainland by a causeway, and it was believed that the building sites there would be sold immediately. This project was largely successful and a number of people settled there until the Depression halted any further development.

In 1930, there were many rumors that the nearby village of Port Washington was about to become a city, as had Glen Cove and Long Beach. The residents of Manhasset Isle feared that if Port Washington did become a city, their village would be annexed. To preserve their independence, therefore, the residents of this village, in addition to those of the small localities of Beach Haven and Orchard Beach on the mainland, decided to incorporate their areas as a separate village. It was reported in September 1930, that "Without one vote in opposition, the property owners who are residents of Manhasset Isle, Beach Haven and Orchard Beach . . . voted to incorporate into a village to be known as Manorhaven."[7] The name Manorhaven was selected by the residents of this area because it was euphonious in its nature. This designation has been in use since the village was incorporated.

Massapequa

The name Massapequa referred originally to the territory inhabited by Indians on the southern portion of Long Island, between what is now Seaford and Islip. In his monumental work on Long Island Indian place-names, William Wallace Tooker gives the variations of this name as Masepeage, Massapeage, Marsapeake, and Messepeake. He defines the name as meaning: "great water land" or "land on the great cove."[1]

The name was used by the settlers in referring to the area so designated today as early as 1658. By 1706, however, the name Oysterbay South had come into existence and was used until 1842.[2] At that time it was transformed to South Oyster Bay, and in 1860, the area was described as: "a scattered village on the south shore."[3]

On July 22, 1887, it was announced that, "The village-to-be of Massapequa has been surveyed and plotted by T. D. Smith, C. E [Consulting Engineer]." The development of this village was principally the work of Thomas H. Brush, who, with several partners, established the Massapequa Improvement Company. They originally purchased three hundred acres of land from the Jones family, located south of Massapequa Lake, and set about improving the area. Money was spent lavishly in grading, dredging the Massapequa River, constructing drives, and other ways to make it a model village for summer residents.[4] At this time Brush was asked if he had selected a name for this development. He replied, "I think of the many names which have suggested themselves to me, I shall settle upon Massapequa."[5]

The name Massapequa became official as the designation of the village in 1889. In January of that year, the Long Island Rail Road Company announced that it would take upon itself the responsibility of changing the title of the South Oyster Bay station to Massapequa.[6] Credit for restoring the name to the area, however, must be given to Thomas H. Brush, and as far as can be ascertained, there have been no attempts to change the name of this village since that time.[7]

Massapequa Park

The Village of Massapequa Park adopted its name from the neighboring village of Massapequa in 1927. The history of this settlement, however, goes back to 1870.

In April of that year, a group of real estate promoters purchased fifteen hundred acres of land and named it Stadt Wurtemberg to attract German settlers.[1] A number of German families did move out to the area from Brooklyn, but eventually the venture failed.[2] The name Stadt Wurtemberg, and later simply Wurtemberg, did continue to be used unofficially, however, until the 1920s.[3]

In 1926, Michael J. Brady learned from Governor Alfred E. Smith of the intended development of Jones Beach. Brady, feeling that a causeway would be built near the Massapequa area, decided it would be a likely location for a model summer village. He enlisted the aid of Frank Cryan and Peter Colleran, and the three partners acquired a fourteen hundred acre tract of land and offered it for sale to the public on November 6, 1927.[4]

According to Michael J. Brady, he selected the name of Massapequa Park because of the site's nearness to Massapequa and because he visualized it as a "Park."[5] The village was incorporated on October 6, 1931, and there have been no attempts to change its name since the village was founded.

Matinecock

The earliest record of this name appears in a document dated April 15, 1644. "*Gauwarowe,* sachem of *Matinnekonck,*" who was acting for the villages of *Matinnekonck, Marospinc,* and *Siketenhacky* "requested to have peace" in their villages.[1] The name, therefore, related to the territory of the Indians who controlled the north shore area from Flushing to the Nissequogue River, as well as to their village.

This name was an Algonquian word descriptive of the area, and the Europeans used it to designate the Indians in the region. William Wallace Tooker stated "this name is descriptive of 'high land,' probably given to one of the many high hills that dot that section—perhaps the high 'Harbor Hill' in North Hempstead. *M'atinne-auke-ut* signifies 'at the place to search, or to look around from,' 'at the place of observation,' 'at the hilly land.'"[2]

In a talk at the Glen Cove Library Lyceum in 1897, George W. Cocks stated that the name Matinecock was then restricted to "the designation of a scattered hamlet between Locust Valley and the Sound," although it had once related to a large area.[3] Eventually, even this small hamlet was absorbed by Locust Valley and Lattingtown and, except for a point of land on Long Island Sound, the name disappeared from the maps.

On April 2, 1928, the residents of an area just south of Locust Valley incorporated their locality as a village. Their reason for doing so was to avoid being included in special districts which would greatly increase their taxes for water, education, and police protection. It then became necessary for them to select a name before they could incorporate as a village. A committee formed for this purpose was composed of Paul D. Cravath, Anton G. Hodenpyl, Paul B. Barringer, Junius S. Morgan, and Sidney Z. Mitchell.[4] This committee wisely selected the very appropriate name of Matinecock, which had been the original Indian name for the entire area.[5]

Merrick

The first recorded use of the name Merrick occurred on December 13, 1643, in the deed selling the land that comprises the Town of Hempstead to Robert Fordham and John Carman. This document stated, "That wee of *Masepeage, Merriack* or *Rockaway* wee hoes [whose] names are hereunder written have sett over and sold unto *Robert Fordham* and *John Carman* on *Long Island* Inglishmen the halfe moiety or equal part of the great plain lying towards the South side."[1]

Among those settlers who came to Hempstead were John Carman and John Smith. There is a legend that both Carman and Smith continued further south from the main settlement, which was to become the village of Hempstead. Supposedly Smith, after arriving at a place which suited him, "threw himself upon the ground among the friendly Indians surrounding him, and declared his intention of here making his home. He asked, 'To what tribe do you belong?' 'Merrick,' was the answer. 'Then,' said Smith, 'we will name the place Merrick, and so it shall ever be.'"[2]

While this legend is undoubtedly fanciful, it is true that Merrick was one of the first areas to be settled after Hempstead and one of the first to be permanently named. It is also true that the name came from the Merrick Indians and the Algonquian geographic description of their land. According to William Wallace Tooker: "This name seems to have been originally applied to the Hempstead plains, which it describes. *Merricock* represents Massachusetts *Mehchi-auke,* 'bare land'; or *Mehchi-auke-ut,* 'at the barren land,' 'bare of trees,' 'a plain.'"[3]

In 1802, this settlement had become large enough for a post office to be established there. For unknown reasons that office was discontinued in 1811, but another was created in August 1843, and has been in continuous existence since that date.[4] No known attempts have been made to change the name of Merrick since it was adopted by the earliest settlers.[5]

Mill Neck

On September 16, 1661, the inhabitants of the Town of Oyster Bay gave Henry Townsend permission to build a mill near the west edge of the village of Oyster Bay. This grant, which appeared in the Town Records, stated:

> Wee doe by these p[r]sents, feremly Covenent & Ingaige, unto Hennery Townesand, now in ye Said Towne on ye Condishtion ye Sd Hennery Townesand, doe Build such a Mill, as at Norwake on ye Maine; or an English Mill, on our Streame called by us ye Mill Revir, at ye west end of our Towne, then doe we gaive & Conferem, Such

Lands to him his heires & assignes for Ever without Molestation or Condishtion.[1]

The river or stream mentioned in this agreement divided the village of Oyster Bay. The neck of land took its name from the river and Townsend's mill and, therefore, became known as Mill River Neck. That appellation first appeared in the Town Records in a deed from Anthony Wright to John Wright, dated May 27, 1698, for land on this neck.[2]

The name Mill River Neck continued to be used in reference to this locality until the late 1700s. The Town Records give the first use of the designation Mill Neck in a deed from Charles Feek to Daniel Cock, Jr., dated June 21, 1788.[3] It was at this time, therefore, that the present-day form of the name, which was descriptive of the peninsula and the fact that one of the town's first mills was located nearby, came into existence.

Mill Neck has been in continuous use as the designation of this area since it was adopted in the 1780s. On March 4, 1925, this village was officially incorporated when the residents of the locality voted in favor of this measure which would ensure their independence.[4]

A nearby locality, which was not included within the limits of the incorporated Village of Mill Neck, has adopted the name of Mill Neck Estates. This section, however, is merely an unincorporated part of the Town of Oyster Bay and is not recognized as an independent village.

Mineola

The area which was to become the Village of Mineola began its development due to the actions of a railroad. Realizing they were losing an important source of revenue by not supplying rail service to the growing village of Hempstead, the Long Island Rail Road Company, which had been incorporated in 1834, decided to build a branch line to Hempstead. After this service was inaugurated in July 1839, a village began to grow at the junction of this branch road and the main line.[1]

This new village immediately became known as Hempstead Branch and undoubtedly was named by the Long Island Rail Road which opened a depot there. This name, however, was never popular with the residents of the area. As early as 1840, a local newspaper referred to the village as being: "commonly called Havilandville."[2] Another article in the same newspaper appeared six years later and stated that Hempstead Branch, "ought properly to have been entitled Havilandville. But as the enterprising proprietor, Isaac E. Haviland, Esq., did not choose to have his name thus transmitted to posterity, I would recommend that steps be immediately taken to have the present odious, unmeaning, term transformed into Titusville, out of respect to the wealthy gentleman who has greatly aided in advancing the interests of the place."[3]

Apparently Mr. Titus also declined to lend his name to the village, for it continued to be known as Hempstead Branch for another twelve years. On June 12, 1858, the Post Office Department officially changed the name of the village to Mineola.[4] However, the railroad continued to use Hempstead Branch as the station name until March 1859.[5] Samuel V. Searing, who resided opposite the site of the railroad depot, was at least in part responsible for the name change, as it was on his petition that the action was taken.[6] Unfortunately, no mention was made as to why the name of Mineola was selected.

Almost paradoxically, the same newspaper which had been advocating a change in names denounced the move after Mineola was selected. It stated: "it is the substitution of a fantastical Indian name for the plain, sensible, significant title which designated that small collection of houses, little known to strangers, but near which passengers to and from this place change cars—Hempstead Branch."[7] Despite this unfriendly reception, the name Mineola has remained the designation of the village since that time, and in 1906, by a majority vote of its residents, Mineola became an incorporated village.

William Wallace Tooker makes no mention of the name Mineola in his work on Long Island Indian place-names. The Bureau of American Ethnology of the Smithsonian Institution stated in 1916, that the name was of Delaware stock: "which in the original was 'Meniolagamike' which signifies 'a pleasant or palisaded village.'"[8]

Munsey Park

Originally the locality that was to become the Village of Munsey Park was considered to be a part of Manhasset. As such it went through the same progression of names as did that village. Therefore, it was first known as a part of Cow Neck, then as Head of Cow Neck, and finally, in June 1837, as Manhasset.[1]

This area was still a part of Manhasset in November 1922, when Frank A. Munsey, publisher of the *Evening Sun* and the *New York Herald,* purchased the Louis Sherry estate. A newspaper reporting this purchase stated: "The Sherry place is one of the show places of this section of Long Island and while the price is not given it is certain that the property cost a considerable sum. . . . The estate comprises 300 acres and the house on it is of French architecture and is built of stone."[2]

Munsey added to this estate by purchasing adjacent tracts of land until it totalled more than six hundred acres. He was, however, in possession of this beautiful estate for a relatively short period of time, as he died on December 22, 1925. Munsey provided wisely for the disposition of this land, since he bequeathed it, in addition to a large part of his forty million dollar fortune, to the Metropolitan Museum of Art.[3]

In gratitude for Munsey's gift, the Metropolitan Museum of Art decided to perpetuate his name by building a model village on this estate. This was to be known as Munsey Park. In 1927, Robert W. deForest, then president of the museum, said: "Although it was apparent from the outset that the museum could not get into the real estate business, it felt something of an obligation to Mr. Munsey's memory to see that the Munsey acres were developed in such a way as to be an asset to the community as well as to the museum."[4]

In 1932, William Sidney Coffin, who was then president of the Metropolitan Museum of Art stated:

> I doubt if there could be found anywhere a community which contains so many authentic replicas of the best and most beautiful in early American architecture and of the most tranquilly charming of Colonial furnishings and decorations.
>
> It would hardly be too much to say that this village is a living extension of the American wing of the Metropolitan Museum of Art, and . . . this was made possible only through the sympathy and ability of the late Robert W. deForest and his associates.
>
> But principally the village is a monument to a man—to the memory of Frank A. Munsey, to whose reasoned and intelligent benefaction the Metropolitan Museum of Art owes so much today. It is built upon part of the estate Mr. Munsey had purchased from the late Louis Sherry and to which he had added other tracts. . . . Mr. Munsey saw in it far more than the attractive features of a rich man's private estate. To him it represented a dream for the future. He saw it as a chance to provide a special kind of comfort and happiness for many people, and at the most moderate cost. . . .
>
> And when Mr. Munsey, in his turn passed along and made the Metropolitan Museum the beneficiary of most of his wealth, including all this land around here, the museum took it upon itself, as a sacred duty, to make Mr. Munsey's dream come true. We wanted to express in this village a sense of our gratitude to Mr. Munsey and our appreciation of what he had done for the museum.[5]

In addition to perpetuating Munsey's name by building this village, the Metropolitan Museum of Art was able to enlarge its art collections through the revenue realized in the sale of houses.[6] By 1930, enough homes had been sold to allow the residents of the area to vote to become an incorporated village under the name of Munsey Park. A few years later the museum severed all its connections with the village by selling its remaining holdings.[7] It did, however, leave one reminder of its association with this village. The names of American artists whose works occupy prominent places in the museum's galleries, such as Hunt, Peale, Copley, Bellows, and Stuart, have been given to Munsey Park's streets.

Munson

The area located between the present-day villages of Franklin Square and West Hempstead had essentially the same background and history as these two places. As it seemed to be most closely related to the present village of Franklin Square, it assumed the use of that village's early names and was known as Trimming Square and Washington Square.

When the area to the west decided to establish a post office in the early 1870s, they were informed that they must change the name of their village. The postal authorities felt that there were too many places in the state already using the name

Washington.[1] For this reason, the residents of that area altered the name of their village to Franklin Square.

The eastern section of this area, however, retained the name Washington Square. When the residents there applied for a post office some twenty years later, the postal authorities again refused the use of the name Washington Square. In May 1895, a meeting was held to select a new name for the village.[2] Those designations suggested were: Munson, Talmageville, and Burnside. It was then agreed to adopt Munson as the new name for this village,[3] in honor of Harry Munson, a Civil War hero who had moved to this area in 1891.[4] A biographical sketch of Munson stated:

> Harry Munson, a well-to-do billposter . . . purchased a small farm at what was known as Franklin Square, L.I., about a year ago. The old farm house was torn down, the low lands filled in and a handsome $30,000 mansion erected back about 300 feet from the Hempstead turnpike, the grounds in front and on either side being terraced and handsomely laid out. . . . So pleased was the people with the bright, genial face of "Harry," as he is known . . . that a petition was largely signed and presented to the postoffice authorities for the changing of the name of the quaint old place to that of "Munson," which was done about six months ago. . . . It is the future purpose of Mr. Munson to erect some 30 or more neat eight room cottages either to let or for sale. . . . From a very poor boy Mr. Munson has arose to a man of great influence and wealth.[5]

In August 1895, the Munson post office opened, and this has been the designation of the village since that date.[6]

Muttontown

The Village of Muttontown appears to have originally been divided between the neighboring areas of Brookville and East Norwich. The first reference to the name Muttontown as a separate locality appeared in the Town Records on October 17, 1781, when the commissioners of highways agreed to establish a road to the common watering springs at that place. The Town Records also refer to Muttontown as "a former great sheep district."[1]

The fact that the designation Muttontown did not seem to have come into use until the final years of the British occupation of Long Island would have made it possible for the English to have created this name which was both descriptive and appropriate at that time. This area continued to use this name at least until 1850, as the Town Records show that on July 12 of that year, Isaac Weeks of Muttontown registered an ear mark for his cattle.[2]

With the decline in the number of sheep being raised in that area, the use of the appellation Muttontown was no longer felt to be appropriate. For that reason, from the 1850s until the village was about to be incorporated in 1931, it was again considered and referred to as being a part of Brookville or East Norwich.[3] This continued to be the situation until many of the residents of this locality expressed a desire to incorporate their village to enable them to establish home rule and maintain its exclusiveness.[4]

For this reason an election was held on July 29, 1931, at the home of David Dows, to decide the issue. This election proved that the residents of the area were definitely in favor of this measure, as they voted unanimously to incorporate their village.[5] After having made this decision, it became necessary to select a name for the new village. Because it had historically been known as Muttontown, and because that name had been preserved by Muttontown Road, it was a logical choice that the old designation be re-adopted. Therefore, the village was officially incorporated as Muttontown in September 1931. This name has been in use since that time.[6]

New Cassel

Records through the mid-1800s refer to the area that was to become the settlement of New Cassel simply as the southeast corner of the Town of North Hempstead.

In the summer of 1870, a development was established there on a site of six hundred acres which had been the farm of Gilbert Baldwin.[1] The neighboring village of Hicksville in the Town of Oyster Bay was primarily populated by residents of German descent. For this reason the developers selected the name New Cassel as a means of attracting additional German immigrants to the area. Cassel (or Kassel) is a city on the Fulda River, and the capital of Hesse, which had united with Prussia in 1866.[2] This proposed development, however, was not successful, and the area remained largely unpopulated for a number of years.

In 1885, a local newspaper stated:

> Perhaps a hundred years from now, when Westbury has grown to be as large as Brooklyn is at present, then that section estimated about two miles east of this station . . . may form one of its beautiful suburbs. At present, however, the prospects are not very inviting. Its wealth lies undeveloped in the yellow sand and the products of its fertile soil is only the scrub-oak. A few years ago an attempt at a settlement was made, but the want of push and enterprise and money, caused the undertaking to be a failure. Those who did settle have long since regretted it and wished themselves elsewhere. A few cling to their places to which they were hurried by false promises and entered upon with such bright hopes, while others have gone and left them go to wreck and ruin.[3]

Despite these warnings, most of the land in this area was purchased by the Buchner Company in 1886. This company, the manufacturers of Gold Coin Chewing Tobacco, gave the name of their product to the locality, which theoretically became Gold Coin City.[4] To publicize their tobacco they began an early form of premium or coupon advertising. It was announced that a building lot at Gold Coin City would be given free for two thousand wrappers from Gold Coin Chewing Tobacco packages.[5]

In April 1891, it was reported that Joshua Romell and Jacob Hicks of Brooklyn, had purchased a large tract of land at New Cassel, to found a village.[6] They proposed to reopen the railroad depot, lay out streets and building lots, and clean up the land. The *East Norwich Enterprise* observed, "With four land companies to boom that vicinity it ought to grow very rapidly."[7]

One of these land companies adopted the name Stewartsville in honor of A. T. Stewart who had founded nearby Garden City. It apparently felt this would increase the value of their property.[8] Neither this name nor Gold Coin City, however, became official, nor was either used for any great length of time. New Cassel, or New Castle as it was occasionally called in error, therefore, has been the official designation of this community since 1870.

New Hyde Park

There is little recorded history prior to 1684, for the locality that is known today as the Village of New Hyde Park. The Town Records indicate that on November 12th of that year, it was voted to give Governor Thomas Dongan two hundred acres of land in the area.[1] Dongan established an estate there and retained ownership of the property until his death in 1698. Governor Dongan died without issue, and the property was inherited by his nephews, Thomas Dongan and Walter Dongan. They sold the estate to George Clarke on August 11, 1724.[2]

Clarke was born at Swanswick in Somersetshire, England, and was a nephew of William Blathwait who held great power over colonial appointments. After completing his training in the law, George Clarke came to America in 1703, as Secretary of the Province of New York. He remained in the province for forty-two years, except for a trip to England in 1705, at which time he married Anne Hyde. During his career here, Clarke became a member of the Provincial Council in 1716, and served as Lieutenant Governor from 1736 to 1743.[3]

Clarke's wife, Anne Hyde, was distantly related to Queen Anne and also to Lord Cornbury, who was then Governor of the Province of New York. In her honor Clarke named his estate Hyde Park. At first this name referred only to Clarke's property, but after he returned to England in 1745, it was used for the entire area.[4] In 1773, however, the section around this estate was referred to as "at Hempstead Plains" and in 1815, as "Plainville."[5] By 1817, the name Hyde Park had been permanently re-established. In that year the noted political writer William Cobbett resided at the former Clarke estate, and his writings, including *A Year's Residence in America,* refer to Hyde Park.[6]

In 1871, John C. Christ and Philip J. Miller applied to the Post Office Department for permission to establish a post office in the village. It was agreed that they could establish one, but the postal authorities refused to allow them to use the name Hyde Park. The reason for this was that a village in Dutchess County had recently adopted the name when they obtained a post office. This village which had been established in 1803 as Crum Elbow, later became famed as the birthplace of Franklin D. Roosevelt.[7]

Christ and Miller were forced, therefore, to settle for New Hyde Park as the name of their village. This appellation was acceptable to the postal authorities, and the Long Island Rail Road changed the name of the station in March 1871.[8] Since that time there have been no attempts to change the name of the village New Hyde Park officially became an incorporated village on August 17, 1927.[9]

North Bellmore

The village of North Bellmore went through the same progression of names as did the village of Bellmore until the mid-1800s. For this reason the area was generally known as Little Neck and after 1818, as New Bridge.[1] By 1850, however, this locality had become known as Smithville, for in March of that year a local newspaper reported, "The dwelling house and store of Mr. Daniel B. Smith, at Smithville near New Bridge, was totally destroyed by fire."[2]

The name Smithville, which apparently had been adopted to honor members of the Smith family who lived there, continued to be used without any attempts to change it until December 1858. At that time a meeting was held by the residents of Little Neck, New Bridge, and Smithville for the purpose of adopting a new designation for the entire area. After electing Stephen Baldwin to act as chairman of this meeting, those present voted to adopt the name of Cedar Valley as the new designation of all three localities. This appellation was never used, however, for another name was selected at a meeting held the following week, and the residents of these villages could not agree upon which should be adopted.[3]

Therefore, the name Smithville continued to be used until 1867, when the residents of this community requested permission to establish a post office there. The postal authorities approved this request, but they insisted that the name of the village be changed because there was already another Smithville in the state. For this reason the name was changed to Smithville South. In April 1867, it was reported that, "A Post Office has been established at Smithville South, Queens County, and Elbert H. Walters has been appointed Post Master."[4]

The name Smithville South continued to be used until the summer of 1919, when the local civic society advocated that this designation be changed. The reason they desired this change was because their mail was being sent to Smithville in Jefferson County, Smithville Flats in Chenango County, and Smithville in Suffolk County. Finally, a local newspaper reported in October 1919:

> Members of the Civic Society and residents generally are highly gratified with the change which the post office department has consented to in designating this place as North Bellmore to succeed Smithville South. The Civic Society petitioned for the change, but was at first turned down. A second petition numerously signed by the residents obtained the desired results.
>
> It is confidently expected that the change will be beneficial generally and will remove the mix-ups in mail and express matter. Besides, it gives the community a railroad designation which was greatly needed.[5]

Although it is known that no attempts have been made to further change the name of this village since it was adopted in 1919, its origin is identical to that of Bellmore and remains unknown at the present time.

North Hills

North Hills, one of Nassau County's more recent villages, was closely identified with its neighboring villages of Searingtown, Manhasset, Plattsdale, and Roslyn, until the 1920s.[1] When many of these localities began to incorporate, this area was not included as a part of any of these municipalities. Fearing that their area would eventually be annexed by another village, the residents of this primarily estate section desired to incorporate their locality before this could happen.[2] Their reason for desiring that status was so they could maintain their independence, and especially so that they could enact their own zoning laws.

For this reason a number of meetings were held to consider this measure, and a petition was circulated calling for an election to decide the issue. The leaders in this movement were Joseph P. Grace, Nicholas Brady, Cornelius Kelly, and Victor Emanuel. With their backing the measure was passed, and the village was officially incorporated in 1929.[3]

When it was originally decided to incorporate this locality, the leaders of the movement realized that it would first be necessary to select a name for the new village. Therefore, the designation of North Hills was decided upon because the area was quite hilly and it was located in the northern part of the county.[4] Since the village was officially incorporated under the name of North Hills, no known attempts have been made to change its descriptive designation.

North Merrick

When the residents of the area directly north of the village of Merrick decided to establish their own post office in 1926, it was necessary for them to select a name for their community. Because of its geographical location and the fact that the area had long been unofficially referred to as North Merrick, it was natural that they should adopt this designation.[1]

In December 1926, when this post office was created, William Jenkins became the first postmaster. He was succeeded by Maude L'Hommedieu and then, in 1930, by Mrs. Charlotte Johnson. According to Mrs. Johnson's son, Norbert Johnson, the post office was located in a real estate office near the corner of Merrick Avenue and Camp Avenue. On December 30, 1933, this post office, which had given an official name to the area, was closed because it was too expensive to maintain. Ironically, Mrs. Johnson died on the same day that the post office was closed.[2]

Alvin Bahnsen, a long time resident of North Merrick, has claimed that Francis Savona devised the name North Merrick when he sent news items of that area to the *Nassau Daily Review-Star*.[3] This would seem improbable, however, as the *Review* and the *Star* did not merge to form the *Nassau Daily Review-Star* until 1937, some eleven years after the creation of the North Merrick post office.

Although postal service for this area has been provided by the Merrick post office since 1934, the name of North Merrick was retained and is still in use.

North New Hyde Park

Although the area known as North New Hyde Park adopted its name solely because of its proximity to the Village of New Hyde Park, it is worthy of notice. In 1858, a local newspaper stated that the residents of that area, "feeling great inconvenience for want of a name to designate the locality have agreed to call it 'Plattsdale.'" This name was chosen to honor Henry W. Platt who was a prominent resident of the area.[1]

The name Plattsdale seems to have gone out of use by 1896, and thereafter this locality was referred to simply as New Hyde Park.[2] In the 1930s and 1940s, new developments such as Hillside Park Oaks, Hillside Lawns, and Hyde Park Manor, came into existence. Because of the increased population created by these developments, it was necessary for the Post Office Department to establish a branch office in that area. This post office was appropriately named North New Hyde Park and opened on December 1, 1958.[3]

Oceanside

The land now comprising the village of Oceanside was given by the residents of the Town of Hempstead to their church to help support its minister.[1] Because the records covering the first ten years of the town's history were lost, it is impossible to tell exactly when the land was granted. The first mention of this property appeared in the Town Records in a lease to John Smith, dated January 16, 1662.[2]

St. George's Episcopal Church (founded 1702) acquired the land. In correspondence, the Reverend Dr. Robert Jenny wrote in 1728, "There belongs to the parsonage a farm, about five miles distant, of one hundred and seventy-two acres of upland and and twenty-five of meadow." In March 1794, the Vestry directed that a portion of this glebe land be sold, but the number of acres involved in this sale was not stated. In 1807, a second sale of these lands was made, and in 1826, the church sold the remainder of its property in this area.[3]

Because of its association with the church and the fact that this land was located on a hook or bend formed by the creek which ran past it, the area became known as Christian Hook at an early but undetermined date. The name Christian Hook was used as the designation of this village until 1880, when it was announced that, "Oceanville is becoming the popular name for our neighboring village of Christian Hook."[4]

Although no immediate action was taken in changing the name of this village, the local newspaper received letters from as far away as Salt Lake City, Utah, protesting any attempt to change the old, honored name of Christian Hook. The following year, however, this same newspaper stated that the name Oceanville was more attractive and that as the village will undoubtedly have a post office, it should have a good, pleasant sounding name. Shortly after this the majority of the residents voted to officially change the designation of their village to Oceanville because the place was near the Atlantic Ocean, and this descriptive name was now more appropriate than Christian Hook.[5]

By 1890, it was being suggested that the name of the village again be changed. At this time it was felt by some residents that Rockville Centre South or Rockville South would be a more appropriate appellation since the village was virtually an extension of Rockville Centre. Finally, in December 1892, a local newspaper reported,

> The Government has established a Post Office in this place and Lorenzo Davison has been appointed Post Master; Lillian Davison, Assistant. The name of the office is "Ocean Side." The application was made for "Oceanville," but the Department claimed that as there are already two Post Offices with that name the mail would be frequently miscarried. The establishment of a post office here is another step in the march of progress for Christian Hook or Oceanville, or Ocean Side. The latter is a good name, and after the office is "running" a while it is likely that Ocean Side will be the name of the place.[6]

By 1896, that designation had evolved into one word, and since then no further attempts have been made to change the name of Oceanside.[7]

Old Bethpage

In 1695, Thomas Powell purchased the area which is today known as Old Bethpage. Like most Quakers, he turned to the Bible to select a name for this property and Bethphage was his choice. The reason for this selection was that this locality was situated between Jericho and Jerusalem, exactly as was the biblical Bethphage.[1] The name first appears in the Town Records in a deed dated June 2, 1697, but eventually, through common usage, it was changed to Bethpage.[2]

This name was used until 1936, with the exception of a small portion of the area which was known as Bedelltown or Beetletown. This designation had been adopted to honor William Beadle, who owned property in this section.[3] In August 1936, however, the area that had been known since 1867 as Central Park began petitioning the Long Island Rail Road Company and the Post Office Department for permission to change the name of their village to Bethpage.[4] When permission was received, and they officially adopted the name Bethpage, the village to the north which had always used this designation was left nameless.

They, therefore, adopted the name Old Bethpage in retaliation for the wrong they felt had been perpetrated upon them. This name became official when the Post Office Department established a branch office there, using that designation in 1965.[5]

Old Brookville

Because the Village of Old Brookville was originally a portion of that area which included the present villages of Brookville and Upper Brookville, it was also a part of the area which was known as Sucos or Suco's Wigwam by the Indians.[1] Of this name, William Wallace Tooker stated that it was, "So called from *Suco*, the Indian who occupied the wigwam. His name is an abbreviation of *Suconamon*, from whom the land was purchased in the early days of the township."[2]

After Captain John Underhill received a grant of land at this place from the Town of Oyster Bay in 1663, the designation of this locality eventually was changed to Wolverhampton. That name first appeared in the Town Records in 1712, and was undoubtedly given to the locality by the Underhill family in honor of their ancestral home in England.[3] Henry C. Shelley, in his biography of Captain John Underhill, stated of the Underhill family in England that, "it was in the southern region of the midland county of Staffordshire, and especially at Wolverhampton and its vicinity, that the most virile and prosperous Underhill family was seated."[4]

By 1768, the name Wolverhampton had been shortened through use or corrupted to Wolver Hollow, and that designation was used continuously until the 1840s.[5] It was announced in February 1848, that the name of this locality was to be changed from Wolver Hollow to Brookville.[6] Apparently this change was not welcomed by all the residents of the area, for several letters appeared in the newspapers protesting this move.[7]

Despite these protests, the name Brookville was adopted and used by the entire area until 1929. In November of that year, it was announced that the property owners in the section near Cedar Swamp Road had issued a petition requesting permission to become an incorporated village. Their purpose in wanting to incorporate was to obtain home rule and freedom from persons residing outside their area. It was also reported in a local newspaper that if the movement was successful, the name of this locality would be changed to the Village of Old Brookville.[8]

The petition was accepted and, at an election held at the house of Herbert L. Budd on December 21, 1929, the residents of the area voted in favor of incorporation by a large majority. Therefore, on December 27, 1929, this part of the Brookville area became officially known as the Village of Old Brookville.[9] Unfortunately, as in the cases of the present-day villages of Brookville and Upper Brookville, the origin of this name has not yet been discovered.

Old Westbury

Wallage, an Indian name, was the first known designation for the present-day Old Westbury area.[1] According to William Wallace Tooker, this word is "related to the Delaware *waloh*, 'a ditch,' 'hole,' 'cave' (*walheu*, 'he digs a hole'). Brinton and Anthony (*Lenâpé Dict.*, 1889) give *walak* or *waleck*, 'a hollow or excavation.'"[2]

The locality eventually was referred to as Wood Edge, and this name first appears in the Town Records in the minutes of a town meeting dated February 9, 1663. On October 2, 1675, Captain John Seaman sold property in this section to Henry Willis.[3] At that time the area was known as "the Plains edge" or

Plainedge.[4] According to Harold Hawxhurst, former village historian of Westbury, it was Henry Willis who gave the area the name Westbury, after a town in his native County of Wiltshire, England.[5] This is quite possible since the designation began to be used in the Town Records on January 16, 1683, eight years after Willis settled in the area.[6]

The name Westbury was continuously used in reference to this locality until the residents of the area attempted to obtain a post office in 1841.[7] At that time it was discovered that a post office with that name had already been established in Cayuga County.[8] It was, therefore, decided to call their post office North Hempstead after the name of the town.[9] Although this was the official name of the post office, the area continued to be known as Westbury. Finally, the residents decided that it was too confusing to have a postal designation that was different from the village name. For this reason they requested that the name of their post office be changed to Old Westbury. This request was granted, and the name of the post office and village officially became Old Westbury in March 1868.[10] For some unknown reason the post office name was changed to Wood Edge on March 13, 1882. This name apparently did not appeal to the residents of the area, and nine days later they managed to have it changed back to Old Westbury.[11]

Since that time there have been no attempts to change the name of this village which was incorporated in 1924. Ironically, the use of the name Westbury in Cayuga County was eventually discontinued, and that designation was adopted by the locality to the south of Old Westbury.[12]

Oyster Bay

One of the oldest non-Indian names in Nassau County is Oyster Bay. The first recorded use of this name occurred in 1639, when David Pietersz De Vries wrote:

> The 4th of June I started north in a yacht to the Fresh River, where the West India Company have a small fort called the House of Hope, and towards evening came to anchor in Oyster Bay, which is a large bay which lies on the north side of the great island, which is about thirty leagues long. This bay runs up into the island, and is about two leagues wide from the mainland. There are fine oysters here, whence our nation has given it the name of Oyster Bay or Harbor.[1]

This descriptive designation was also adopted by the village which soon grew on the edge of the harbor. The use of the name Oyster Bay continued until January 5, 1846, at which time the designation of the post office located there was changed to Syosset.[2] In writing of the adoption of that name a local newspaper stated, "One of the prettiest villages on Long Island, has, for many years been disfigured under the name of Oyster, or Clam Bay. The inhabitants have recently restored its ancient and euphonical Indian name of Syosset, and the Postmaster General has consented to the change."[3]

The idea that Syosset had been the Indian name for the site of Oyster Bay village has been suggested. William Wallace Tooker, however, rejected this theory and stated that Syosset "is of Indian derivation: it has been evolved from the Dutch *Schouts,* 'a sheriff.' *Schout, Siocits, Syocits,* are some of the various stages of degradation down to its present form.'[4]

This change of names was vigorously opposed by the older residents of the village and the name Oyster Bay was supposedly restored after one week. It took longer to get the name of the post office restored, but that was finally accomplished on July 31, 1848.[5] Syosset was later adopted as the designation of the village which now bears that name. Except for this brief period, therefore, the village of Oyster Bay has always been known by the name the Dutch explorers had bestowed upon it.[6]

Oyster Bay Cove

The Village of Oyster Bay Cove takes its name from the village and harbor of Oyster Bay and from the fact that it is located on a small cove that leads into the harbor. The descriptive designation Oyster Bay Cove, or simply The Cove, appeared in the Town Records as early as April 9, 1681, and has continued in use to this date.[1]

During the 1920s and early 1930s, the villages of Bayville, Brookville, Centre Island, Cove Neck, Laurel Hollow, Matinecock, Mill Neck, and Muttontown, which surrounded Oyster Bay Cove, were officially incorporated. The reason these villages took this action was to preserve their home rule and be able to enact their own zoning regulations. The Village of Oyster Bay Cove soon became motivated by the same desire to ensure its independence. On November 11, 1931, therefore, Supervisor Benjamin W. Downing granted the residents of the area permission to hold a public election on the proposition to incorporate their village.[2] This proposition was approved and on December 29, 1931, the Village of Oyster Bay Cove was officially incorporated under the name which had been used since the area was first settled.[3]

Plainedge

The first known use of the name Plainedge or Plain Edge was in reference to the locality which is now known as the Village of Old Westbury. This appellation appeared in the Town Records when Captain John Seaman sold property there to Henry Willis on October 2, 1675.[1] That same area had also been known as Wood Edge, and the origin of these names was obviously the fact that the place was situated on the northern edge of the Hempstead Plains.[2] The village of Plainview was to receive its name for the same reason, and eventually the present village of Plainedge also adopted its designation because it was near the eastern edge of the plains.

Originally this area was considered to be a part of the Bethpage purchase and was generally known by that name.[3] When the various localities there began to assume separate identities as they became settled, they adopted individual names. It is impossible to say with any certainty when this area received Plainedge as its first name. However, it is known that it was being referred to as Turkeyville by the early 1800s.[4] It is also known that the name Plain Edge or

Plainedge first appeared in the Town Records on February 12, 1814, in relation to redesignating the boundaries of the school districts in the Town of Oyster Bay.[5]

In referring to these names, Nathaniel S. Prime stated in 1845:

> *Plain Edge,* or *Turkeyville,* is a settlement lying partly in Oyster-bay, and partly in Hempstead, between 3 and 4 miles from the south road, and about the same distance south of Hicksville. . . . Either of the above names is sufficiently distinctive. The village is situated on the verge of the Great Plain, whence its ancient name originated. And while the land is excellent, and, in general, well cultivated, the inhabitants excel in the art of raising *turkeys.* In passing through this vicinity, you behold immense flocks of these fowls, spreading over the fields, and often extending their stroll out upon the plain. Thousands of these are annually raised in this vicinity; and on that account, the very appropriate name was applied to it, by one of the oldest inhabitants.[6]

The designation of Turkeyville seems to have gone out of existence shortly after 1845, as it does not appear in print after that date. This name was never used in reference to the school district located there as it undoubtedly was not thought to be a very appropriate appellation. For this reason the name Plainedge has been in constant use since that time, although sections of Plainedge were known as Frog Hollow and Bloomingdale for brief periods.[7]

Plainview

Manetto Hill was the Indian appellation by which the present-day village of Plainview was originally known. The first recorded use of this name appeared in the Town Records in a deed dated August 18, 1695.[1]

Gabriel Furman gives the traditional account of the origin of this name as follows:

> About thirty miles from Brooklyn, and midway between the north and south sides of this island, is a hill known by the name of *Manet,* or *Manetta Hill.* This, however, is a corruption of the true name, which was *Manitou Hill,* or the Hill of the Great Spirit; which appellation is founded on the tradition, that many ages since, the aborigines residing in those parts suffered extremely from the want of water. Under their suffering they offered up prayers to the Great Spirit for relief. That in reply to their supplications, the Good Spirit directed that their principal chieftain should shoot his arrow into the air, and on the spot where it fell they should dig, and would assuredly discover the element they so much desired. They pursued the direction, dug, and found water. There is now a well situated on this rising ground, which is not deep, and the tradition continues to say that this well is on the very spot indicated by the Good Spirit. This hill was undoubtedly used in ancient times as the place of general offering to the Great Spirit in the name and behalf of all surrounding people; and was of the character of the hill-altars so common among the early nations. It is from this circumstance that the name was most probably derived.[2]

Of the meaning of the name of Manetto Hill, William Wallace Tooker stated:

> The name signifies "a hill surpassing others in the same vicinity," being derived from *mon,* "surpassing," and *attin,* "a hill," hence "the surpassing or wonderful hill." Mount *Monadnock* in New Hampshire gets its name from *Mon-adn-ock,* ("land or country of the surpassing mountain"; *mon,* "surpassing"; *adn,* "hill or mountain"; *ock, auke,* "land or country"), being thus a parallel to *Mannatto.*[3]

The designation Manetto Hill was used until the residents of that locality requested permission to establish a post office in 1885. Although the postal authorities were willing to grant their permission, they would not accept the name Manetto Hill. Their reason for this refusal was that there was already a post office in New York State known as Maintou, and they feared the similarity of these names would cause confusion.[4]

For this reason the residents of the community adopted the descriptive designation of Plainview, because the Hempstead Plains stretched out for sixteen miles to the west and could be seen for almost their entire distance from this locality. In March 1886, a local newspaper reported that the name of this village had been changed to Plainview, and since that date this designation has been in continuous use.[5]

Plandome

Although the area which today comprises the Village of Plandome was closely related to its neighboring village of Manhasset and was generally known by that village's designations, it did have a history of its own. In 1670, Matthias Nicoll, the first English secretary of New York, had purchased land in that locality. The Town of Hempstead later gave Nicoll an additional two hundred acres adjoining the lands he had purchased. At the time of his death in 1690, his property there totalled some twelve hundred acres.[1]

In 1718, William Nicolls sold this property to Joseph Latham for £2,350. Eventually these lands were left to Dr. Samuel Latham who, although a bachelor, was responsible for raising his nephew and namesake, Dr. Samuel Latham Mitchill.[2] When Latham died, he left his lands in this area to Mitchill. It is to him that the Village of Plandome owes its name.

Mitchill, who was well versed in Latin, gave his home the name of Planus Domus or plain home. This designation, which eventually became the name of the entire area was corrupted to Plandome.[3] Henry Onderdonk, Jr. appears to have discovered the earliest use of that name for he recorded, as of October 10, 1806, "Died at Plandome, aged 69, of an apoplectic fit, Mary Latham relict of the late Robert Mitchell and mother of Dr. S. L. Mitchell, Senator to the United States."[4]

From the early 1800s, therefore, this area was generally known as Plandome or Plandome Mills, in reference to the mill which the Latham and Mitchill families operated at that place.[5] When it was decided to incorporate this village in 1911, there does not seem to have been any question but that its name should be Plandome. Since that date the name has been the official designation of this village. Plandome must be said to be a euphonious appellation, as the name Mitchill gave to his home could hardly be declared to be descriptive of the area or any of its features.

Plandome Heights

The Village of Plandome Heights, located between the villages of Manhasset and Plandome, was long identified with the village of Manhasset. For this reason the entire area was known as Cow Neck. That name first appeared in the Town Records in an agreement dated April 23, 1669.[1] When a settlement began to grow at the site of the village of Manhasset, it became known as Head of Cow Neck.

The name Head of Cow Neck, or simply Cow Neck, continued to be used until 1837, at which time this designation was felt by the residents of the village to be no longer appropriate. After considering a number of names, including Plandome, Millport, Locust Branch, and Robinia, the committee which had been formed to select the new designation decided that Manhasset would be a suitable appellation. In June 1837, therefore, Manhasset became the name of this community, and it has been in continuous use since that time.[2]

Despite the fact that Plandome had become the name of the settlement to the north of this locality by 1806, no attempt was made to disassociate itself from the village of Manhasset until the early 1900s.[3] At that time most of the present Plandome Heights area was owned by the Duke family.[4] They formed a corporation to develop the land, and a map was filed on January 10, 1910, referring to the area as Plandome Heights.[5] Since that date this euphonious designation has been used for this village without interruption.

The Plandome Heights Corporation, which developed the locality for the Duke family, proved successful in its efforts, and a number of new residents settled there. By 1929, it was felt by these new residents that the village should be incorporated to protect its exclusiveness. Therefore, in February of that year, a petition was circulated requesting that this locality be annexed or added to the Village of Plandome.[6] When the request failed to gain approval, an election was held to incorporate the area as a separate village to be known as Plandome Heights. This move proved successful, and the village was officially incorporated on June 11, 1929.[7]

Plandome Manor

The early history of the area which was to become the Village of Plandome Manor was virtually identical to that of its neighboring villages of Plandome and Plandome Heights. Like the Village of Plandome Heights, this locality began to be developed in the early 1900s, under the separate name of Plandome Park.[1] Although that development did not prove too successful, the name was still in existence in the early 1920s, and a new section, known as Plandome Estates, was also being promoted.[2]

These separate ventures eventually combined under the present designation of Plandome Manor, and the area began to assume the exclusive qualities it now possesses. In August 1932, it was announced that a group known as the Plandome Manor Association had been formed, at the home of Walter A. Morris, to solve the problems affecting the property owners.[3] Apparently these problems, which included taxes, lighting, roads, and schools for the area, proved too complex for a private group to solve. Later in that year, therefore, the residents of the community voted to officially incorporate their village under the name of Plandome Manor.[4]

Point Lookout

Although the community of Point Lookout is of recent origin when compared to many other villages in Nassau County, its name dates back to the early 1700s. This locality on the eastern end of Long Beach island, was constantly changing in size and appearance as the present Jones Inlet moved westward and the sand, of which it was composed, was eroded by the winds and ocean currents. This area, however, was occasionally inhabited by fishermen and whalers, and they created the name by which it is now known.[1]

Daniel M. Tredwell, in writing of Long Island whaling in the colonial period, stated that a number of whales were taken from the waters off the south shore during the 1600s and early 1700s. Because of the profits derived from this industry, the whalers established stations along the shore to maintain a constant watch for these whales. By 1721, "A lookout and station for whalemen was maintained at Whale Neck and another at Long Beach opposite the Hummocks near New Inlet."[2] The description of this locality, south of the Hummock and near New Inlet or present-day Jones Inlet, corresponds exactly to Point Lookout. That there was a lookout station there and since this area was at the easterly point of Long Beach island, the name Point Lookout is particularly descriptive.

The United States Life Saving Service, later to become part of the United States Coast Guard, established a station there in the late 1800s.[3] In searching for a name for this station they re-adopted Point Lookout. This eventually became the designation for the entire east end of Long Beach island.

During the early 1900s, a summer colony was begun in this area by the Nassau Cottage and Realty Company. By 1904, it was noted that there were twenty-seven cottages or bungalows in this development which had been named Nassau-by-the-Sea.[4] This popular colony was all but wiped out in May 1918, when it was reported:

> Fire on Friday swept the summer bungalow colony at Nassau-by-the-Sea, on the eastern end of Long Beach, known as Point Lookout. Meyer's Hotel, a two-story building, forty one-story bungalows, the Post Office building, the boardwalk and a number of other structures were destroyed.[5]

The post office that was destroyed by this fire must have been the Point Lookout office which had been established in May 1906.[6] When the post office was opened, Point Lookout became the official name of this village. In effect, however, this name has been in use since the whaling station was established there in the early 1700s.

Port Washington

Originally the entire area from Manhasset north to Sands Point was known as Cow Neck. This name was first used in the Town Records in an agreement dated April 23, 1669, referring to a fence which had been built across the base of this peninsula.[1] With the addition of this fence, it became a natural pasture for the cattle owned by the residents of the town, and for this reason received this rather bucolic name.

The site of present-day Port Washington, however, had previously been known by the Indian name of Sintsinck. This designation was first recorded in an Indian deed dated January 15, 1639, which stated, "We Director and Council of *New Netherland* etc., testify and declare that to-day . . . personally appeared before us *Mechowodt,* chief Sachem of *Marossepinck, Sintsinck,* (also called Schouts bay) and its dependances."[2] Algonquianist William Wallace Tooker stated, "This name is probably the same as *Sing-Sing* in Westchester Co., N.Y. Originally this was *Ossining,* said to signify 'stone upon stone,' that is, 'a stony place.' In 1901 the old name Ossining was readopted. For this name another etymology *assinesink* 'at the little stone,' has been offered."[3]

By 1761, however, the bay upon which this settlement is located began to be referred to as Cow Bay.[4] The name gradually began to be applied to the growing village, and it also became known as Cow Bay. This designation was used until 1859, at which time it was decided to establish a post office in the village.[5] This decision apparently led the residents of the area to feel that this would be an appropriate time to choose a new name for their village.

Because George Washington had passed this area on his tour of Long Island in 1790, it was decided to honor the country's first president by adopting his name.[6] Rather than just call their village Washington, it was decided to also use the word "Port" to signify the area's marine background.[7] The name Port Washington, therefore, was the designation submitted to the Post Office Department by Thomas McKee and Elbert Mackey, when they applied for permission to establish a post office in the village.[8] On July 2, 1859, a local newspaper stated: "The name of the locality known as Cow Bay . . . has been changed to Port Washington. We understand that application has been made with the view to establish a Post Office at this place. . . . Under the new name the locality will no doubt flourish and prosper."[9]

This name has been continuously used since that date, and no known attempt has been made to further alter it. In March 1932, an attempt to incorporate this village failed, and this area has remained an unincorporated part of the Town of North Hempstead.[10]

Port Washington North

The history of the incorporated Village of Port Washington North was identical to that of the village of Port Washington until the early 1930s. At that time other sections which had originally been a part of Port Washington, such as Baxter Estates and Manorhaven, began to incorporate as independent villages.[1]

When these areas withdrew from the unincorporated village of Port Washington, it began the dissolution of the area's water district and encouraged various portions of the village to request annexation by bordering incorporated villages. In March 1932, therefore, a movement was begun to join all the remaining parts of Port Washington into an incorporated village. Judge Cortland A. Johnson, however, declared this plan to be illegal as these areas were not contiguous, being separated by Baxter Estates and Manorhaven.[2]

For this reason, the residents of the section located north of the main portion of Port Washington requested permission to create a new incorporated village to be known as Port Washington North. This name was selected simply because the area was geographically north of Port Washington.[3]

Papers filed with Supervisor Charles Snedeker showed the area to include the property of Jacob Cocks, the Crescent Sand and Gravel Company, the Millpond section, and part of the development that was known as Hicksville. This was the area the Village of Manorhaven had attempted to annex the year before. This attempt had failed, however, because the people who lived there preferred to form a village of their own.[4]

On July 6, 1932, the residents of this area voted unanimously in favor of incorporating their village. Jacob Cocks, who had led this movement, was elected the first mayor of this village on August 2, 1932.[5] The name Port Washington North has been in constant use since the time this village came into existence.

Rockville Centre

Originally a part of that large area known as Near Rockaway, this locality began to assume a separate identity in 1790. In that year the Sand Hole Methodist Church was constructed to serve the small community of farmers who had settled there.[1] This community continued to grow, and in the 1840s the first store in the area was constructed by Robert Pettit.[2]

Pettit, who wanted to establish a post office in the locality, realized that it first would be necessary to select a name for the community.[3] A local newspaper attested to the fact that this was accomplished by reporting, "At a public meeting held at Near Rockaway on Saturday, the 21st day of August, 1847, pursuant to public notice, it was resolved that the neighborhood and vicinity of the Methodist Meeting House at Near Rockaway, on both sides of the stream, should be hereafter known and designated by the name of 'Rockville.'"[4]

The name Rockville had been selected by the area's residents to honor the Reverend Mordecai Rock Smith, the village's popular minister. Unfortunately, this designation was not acceptable to the postal authorities as there was already another Rockville in the state in Orange County.[5] The names Smithtown, Smithfield, and Smithberg were then offered, but they were also rejected on the same grounds. Finally the word "Centre" was added to Rockville, the original name that had been proposed, and this designation was accepted by the Post Office Department.[6]

In February 1849, a local newspaper stated that: "A new Post Office has been authorized at Rockville, formerly Near Rockaway, and Robert Pettit, Esq. has been appointed Post Master. We understand the Mail is to be carried daily to and from this village." This statement was corrected the following week, when this newspaper announced, "The article published in the Inquirer of last . . . . appears to have conveyed a wrong impression, to the minds of some of our readers, as to the locality of the Office. The place where the new office is established, is not at Rockville, as some suppose, but at Rockville Centre, which is a mile and a half distant from the former place."[7]

The name Rockville Centre was used without incident until 1882, at which time a movement was begun to change the name of the village. The reason for this movement was that some of the residents felt the name Rockville Centre was too long and awkward. The name Davison was then suggested as an alternative, to honor the many members of that family who lived in the village. A meeting was held at Institute Hall on June 6, 1882, at which time it was decided by a large majority to retain the name Rockville Centre.[8]

Despite the fact that Rockville Centre officially became an incorporated village under that designation on July 15, 1893, a final attempt was made to change its name.[9] This occurred in October 1924, but an apparent lack of interest on the part of the village's residents ended this movement.[10] The village has, therefore, continued under the name it adopted in 1849.[11]

Roosevelt

The area located midway between the villages of Hempstead and Freeport was sparsely settled until the early 1800s. At that time the future village was known by the colloquial name of Rum Point, because three of its fifteen buildings were taverns, and they were situated at its main intersection.[1]

In 1845, the historian Nathaniel S. Prime described the village as follows:

> On the south road about 3 miles south-east of the village of Hempstead, is a small neighborhood, which has long borne the name of *Rum Point*. Why such a forbidding appellation was applied, the writer is not informed. Recent efforts have been made to change the name to Greenwich, which the village-landlord has mounted upon his sign. But, as the writer, in making a recent excursion through this neighborhood, saw *three* men, literally reeling through the street, he was inclined to believe that the old name was the most appropriate.[2]

Although the reason for the selection of Greenwich or Greenwich Point as the new designation for this village does not seem to have been recorded, it is known that it was definitely in use by 1860. A gazetteer published in that year refers to Greenwich Point as being a farming neighborhood located to the west of the village of Merrick.[3]

The name Greenwich Point was used until 1902, at which time the residents of the village applied for permission to establish a post office. While this application was approved, the postal authorities stated that a new name would have to be selected. The reason for this was that there was already another village in the state using Greenwich as the designation for their post office.[4]

A meeting was held, therefore, at the store of Royal Mollineaux, one of the leading candidates for the position of postmaster. Those present at this meeting, which was held on February 12, 1902, voted to change the name of the village to Royalston. A local newspaper in reporting this decision stated, "While the name of Royalston would be very appropriate, and a neat compliment to Mr. Royal Mollineaux, a prominent merchant there, a great many of the residents favor the name of Laramie."[5] Despite this vote in favor of Royalston as the new designation of their village, the majority of the residents were not in favor of either this name or Laramie. Another vote was taken, and the name Roosevelt was adopted, in honor of President Theodore Roosevelt.[6]

This name seemed particularly appropriate, for in addition to being president, Roosevelt was also a resident of Nassau County. The new designation was accepted by the Post Office Department and permission to establish a post office in the village was granted on March 1, 1902.[7] The name Roosevelt has been in continuous use since that date, and there have been no further attempts to rename this village.

Roslyn

The Town Records first mention the name Hempstead Harbor in relation to the body of water that still bears this name. This designation apparently evolved because it was the nearest harbor to the Village of Hempstead. The first reference in the Town Records to the settlement that grew at the head of this harbor is a deed dated 1709.[1] This settlement was originally referred to as Head of Hempstead Harbor, but eventually this laborious name was shortened to simply Hempstead Harbor.

The designation Hempstead Harbor in reference to this village was used until 1844, at which time the residents of the area felt it was necessary to change the name. The reasons for this action were described in a notice which appeared in a local newspaper. It stated that the inhabitants of Hempstead Harbor were inconvenienced because of the similarity of the names Hempstead, North Hempstead, Hempstead Branch, and Hempstead Harbor. This similarity of names was causing their mail to be sent to other localities, and for this reason they announced that they had selected Roslyn as the new designation of their village. This notice was signed by forty-two property owners, including William Cullen Bryant.[2]

In a letter to historian Benjamin F. Thompson, dated September 2, 1844, Ebenezer Close, one of the signers of the above mentioned notice, described the method of selecting a new name for the village as follows:

> I received soon after its date your polite note containing a list of names which you suggest as suitable for the village of Hempstead Harbour. This letter . . . I submitted to Mr. Bryant and Mr. Leggett; and on Saturday Evening Mr. Leggett invited such gentlemen as had taken most interest in this affair to meet at his house to determine what

name to submit to the inhabitants for their approval. By a Rule which we had adopted but a few of the names could be admitted at all. We wanted a short name of soft pleasant sound; one that would do away with the word "Harbour," and one that had not been appropriated as the name of any Post Office in the United States. The first part of our Rule shut out nearly all the Indian names; the second, all those ending in "port" or "haven";—and the third nearly all the rest. . . . Ten names . . . were submitted to be balloted for; when the name "Roslyn" was found to have the greatest number of votes, and was afterwards unanimously approved by all who were present. We signed our names to a paper expressing that approbation, which will now be submitted to the inhabitants generally for signature.[3]

William Cairns who attended this meeting is said to have suggested the name Roslyn because the village and surrounding area reminded him of Roslyn, Scotland.[4] Despite this evidence a legend has grown that: "the village was named Roslyn because of the unhappy love affair of a village girl who failed to escape with her soldier lover when his Scottish Regiment left the 'Harbor' at the end of the Revolutionary War with bagpipes playing 'Roslin Castle,' a popular song of the day."[5]

In October 1844, the Post Office Department accepted the change in the name of the village to Roslyn, and since that time there have been no further efforts to alter it.[6] On January 11, 1932, Roslyn officially became an incorporated village.[7]

Roslyn Estates

According to Louis O. Rohland, former village historian of Roslyn Estates, a group was formed to develop this section in 1908, under the name of Roslyn Estates Incorporated.[1] This appears to be the first use of the name Roslyn Estates for this area, which previously had taken the designations Hempstead Harbor and Roslyn from its neighboring village to the north.

Their development of this locality was successful and in 1911, the Association of Roslyn Estates was formed by the residents of the newly established village.[2] This group, which still exists, helped formulate community actions in lieu of any other regulating agency. When the original deed restrictions were about to expire, however, the residents took steps to incorporate their village. Incorporation of the Village of Roslyn Estates, therefore, became a reality on June 8, 1931.[3]

It is apparent that this village took its name directly from the Roslyn Estates Incorporated, the group which developed the area. As with Roslyn Harbor and Roslyn Heights, this name can indirectly be traced through the neighboring village of Roslyn, to Roslyn, Scotland.

Roslyn Harbor

The section that was to become the incorporated Village of Roslyn Harbor was originally a portion of that area known as Hempstead Harbor. After the Village of Roslyn received its present name in 1844, this area adopted that as its designation.[1] Therefore, although officially outside the actual limits of that village, this section was generally referred to as Roslyn.

In the early 1930s it was decided to incorporate this locality, which was then composed primarily of the estates of Childs Frick, Mrs. F. H. Goddard, and P. R. Pyne.[2] This was done so that the residents would be able to establish their own zoning laws and maintain restrictions that had been imposed on the use of this section's lands. Before incorporation of the locality became official on October 17, 1931, it was necessary to select a name for the new village.[3]

A meeting was held for that purpose and Conrad Godwin Goddard has written that:

> Because the name "Roslyn" was very well known, it was obvious that we should use that word as a part of the new designation, so that everyone would know where we were located. One suggestion was to call the village "Roslyn Hills." This seemed at first appropriate, since in the early literature of the Long Island Railroad this district was referred to as the "Switzerland of Long Island." Yet it was pointed out by some of the incorporators that the term "Hills" might become confused with the already existing Village of Roslyn Heights. So, at the suggestion of my cousin Miss Elizabeth Love Godwin, also a great-grandchild of William Cullen Bryant, the Village Board adopted instead the name "Roslyn Harbor" as more appropriate, since the area lay for its entire length along the harbor.[4]

This name suggested by Miss Godwin has been in continuous use since the village was incorporated and no attempts to change it have been made.

Roslyn Heights

The present-day village of Roslyn Heights was originally referred to as a part of Hempstead Harbor and later of Roslyn. In 1892, a corporation was formed to develop this section under the name of Roslyn Highlands.[1] The leading members of this corporation were: Eugene D. Berri, President of the Standard Land Company; T. W. Lawrence, a lawyer; Paul E. DeFere, Secretary of the Citizen's Real Estate Company; Henry E. Hutchinson, President of the Brooklyn Bank; Camden C. Dike, of the Kings County Bank; Henry B. Platt; and E. M. Lindgren, Treasurer of the Mineola Park Company.[2]

Despite their impressive qualifications, these men were unable to successfully develop this area. The property, which consisted primarily of the Maple Hill, Appleby, and Pearsall farms, was later transferred to the Dean Alvord Company.[3] It developed the area in two sections, with the westerly part retaining the name Roslyn Highlands and the easterly tract becoming known as Roslyn Heights.[4] These two names remained until the late 1920s, at which time the entire locality became known as Roslyn Heights. Possibly this was because the area had received its post office on July 18, 1913, under that name. However, the fire department has continued to be known as the Roslyn Highland Hook and Ladder Company.[5] This area, which never incorporated, can trace its name back to

Roslyn, Scotland, as can the Villages of Roslyn, Roslyn Estates, and Roslyn Harbor.

Russell Gardens

Francis H. Knighton, the founder of the Village of Russell Gardens, had been associated in a minor way with the Rickert-Finlay Realty Company, which had developed the Village of Kensington.[1] This experience left him with the desire to develop a village of his own.

In searching for property for this village, Knighton remembered the Captain Frederick Russell estate on Northern Boulevard in Great Neck. Knighton was well acquainted with this area as he had stabled a thoroughbred riding horse there. He persuaded Captain Russell to sell his land except for a small portion near the corner of Northern Boulevard and Middle Neck Road where his house was located. Knighton also purchased additional acreage from Arthur Cushman, the bakery magnate, and others.[2]

The Russell property had been owned by the Schenck family for many generations and then by the Haviland family before Russell acquired it in 1893. Captain Russell, who had named his property Russell Harbour, was a noted character in the Great Neck area. His likeness to George Bernard Shaw was so remarkable that it even amazed Shaw. On one occasion when the noted playwrite visited Great Neck, he was constantly mistaken for Captain Russell. Eventually, Russell won a sort of international fame when British magazines published their pictures together as doubles.[3]

After having acquired a total of 135 acres of land, which is the size of the present village, Knighton began to develop the area. One of the first acts taken by Knighton was to name the area Russell Gardens in honor of Captain Russell.[4] When he decided to incorporate the syndicate that was helping him to finance this operation, it became Russell Gardens, Inc.

This group laid out the streets, parks, had all wiring placed underground, and engaged J. J. Levinson, the famed landscape gardener, to beautify the property.[5] The houses constructed there proved to be very popular, and the development became a great success. To preserve the beautiful character of their community, the residents realized it would be necessary to pass their own zoning ordinances. For this reason Russell Gardens officially became an incorporated village in 1931, and it has continued under the name it was given when the development was first begun.[6]

Saddle Rock

Undoubtedly the most unusual geological feature in the area which now comprises the Village of Saddle Rock was a large out-cropping of rock situated near the shore in Little Neck Bay. This rock was named Saddle Rock because it resembled a high-pommeled saddle. However, it is not mentioned in the Town Records, so it is not possible to ascertain when this designation came into use.

Like all villages on the Great Neck peninsula, this community was originally known as a part of Madnans Neck, that name first appearing in the Town Records in a deed dated January 8, 1668. The designation Madnans Neck did not remain in use for long, as a deed to Robert Jackson dated March 8, 1672, shows that it had been replaced by the name Great Neck.[1] That appellation continued to be used for most of this locality until the various communities on this neck began to assume separate identities and individual names.

The first known owner of property in the Saddle Rock area appears to have been Robert Hubbs, who settled there in the 1690s.[2] Hubbs sold this land to Henry Allen in 1702, and it remained in the possession of his family for many years. Eventually this property passed into the hands of the Udall family. In the 1830s, it was acquired by the Skidmore family who owned it until it was inherited by Mrs. Roswell Eldridge, née Skidmore.[3] Mr. and Mrs. Eldridge continued to own most of this land until after the community became the first incorporated village on the Great Neck peninsula.

This incorporation took place on January 3, 1911, and at that time the name Saddle Rock was re-established as it was distinctive and highly descriptive of this unusual rock located only a few yards off the shore. With the incorporation of the village, Roswell Eldridge became its first mayor. He continued in that post until his death in the 1920s. Thereafter, his widow, Louise Udall Eldridge, became mayor of the village and was the first woman to hold that office in Nassau County.[4] Since this village was established, there have been no attempts to change its name.

The nearby area of Saddle Rock Estates was not included within the boundaries of this community when it was incorporated. Although it took its name from the Village of Saddle Rock, it has no official connection with that village and is merely an unincorporated portion of the Town of North Hempstead.

Sands Point

The entire area from Sands Point south to Manhasset was originally known by the settlers as Cow Neck. This name which first appeared in the Town Records on April 23, 1669, was adopted because this peninsula or neck of land was used for grazing the cattle owned by the residents of the town.[1] The first known settler in the northern area of the peninsula was Richard Cornwell, who purchased land there in 1679. Cornwell eventually moved to Rockaway and on December 25, 1691, he sold his property on Cow Neck to John Sands.[2]

Originally the Sands family had resided at Block Island, where John Sands' father owned considerable land. Sands, who was born in 1669, migrated to Long Island with his brothers James and Samuel. Because of his close connection with the sea dating back to his early life at Block Island, John Sands became a sea captain, trading between New York and Virginia. On one of his trips to the south he brought back a number of small locust trees which he introduced to this area. Sands lived on his property at the tip of Cow Neck until his death on March 15, 1712.[3]

Following Captain John Sands' death, this property passed through the hands of many members of his family. The name Sands Point, however, does not seem to have come into use until the late 1790s. By 1809, when the lighthouse was constructed at that place, the locality was definitely known as Sands Point.[4] The first use of this name in the Town Records, however, did not occur until 1818.[5]

Little change took place in this locality through the nineteenth century. By the early 1900s, however, the construction of large estates had begun at Sands Point. The new residents of this section eventually decided that they should incorporate their area to ensure its exclusive qualities. For this reason, the Sands Point area and the adjoining localities of Barker's Point and Mott's Point published a notice expressing their intention to incorporate as three separate villages.[6] Like Sands Point, Barker's Point and Mott's Point had taken their names from the early settlers of those sections. These attempts to incorporate failed, but then they joined together and, under the name Sands Point, became an incorporated village on July 23, 1912.[7]

Sea Cliff

When Joseph Carpenter purchased the site of Glen Cove in 1668, he also acquired the land that was to become the future Village of Sea Cliff. The Indians, however, disputed the fact that they had sold this area, and they resold it in January 1681, to Richard Kirby, George Downing, Jacob Brookin, and Robert Godfree.[1] This purchase was soon confirmed for a fee by the proprietors of Glen Cove, and the new locality became known as Littleworth.[2]

The name Littleworth first appeared in the Town Records in an acknowledgement of a payment from Richard Kirby dated January 31, 1683.[3] Littleworth was probably applied to this locality because one of the first settlers had originally come from the village of that name in England, rather than because this property was felt to be of little value.

This locality continued to be known as Littleworth, as may be seen in the Town Records, until at least the 1830s.[4] After that period this area began to be referred to as Carpenterville. The reason that designation came into use was that the Carpenter family, descendants of Joseph Carpenter, owned virtually the entire area. The last member of that family to own this property was James S. Carpenter who sold it to the Camp Ground Association of New York and Brooklyn in 1871, for four hundred dollars an acre.[5]

The Metropolitan Camp Ground Association of New York and Brooklyn had been incorporated on October 12, 1871, shortly before it purchased the former Carpenter farm. The reasons this corporation was formed were declared to be:

> The erection of buildings for meetings for religious purposes, and for the accommodation of those who shall attend them; the acquiring of the necessary ground and land therefor, and the erection thereon of suitable buildings, cottages, and improvements for meetings, dwellings, boarding-houses, shelter and other purposes connected with the general objects of such society.[6]

Their plan was to provide a healthful summer resort for Christian families. They named their new property Sea Cliff Grove because it was descriptive of the locality, which was situated on a wooded bluff by the sea.[7] As soon as the Camp Ground began its summer operations in the early 1870s, a village began to grow about it which was known simply as Sea Cliff. By 1883, the village was officially incorporated under the name of Sea Cliff, and no further attempts have been made to change its designation.[8]

Seaford

The first name for the extreme southeast corner of the Town of Hempstead appears to have been Jerusalem South. The name was shared by this area and its neighboring community to the west, which was to become the village of Wantagh. On April 7, 1838, it was announced that a new post office to be known as Jerusalem South had been established to serve both of these areas.[1]

The name Jerusalem South was officially used for this locality until the South Side Railroad of Long Island completed its line through the present-day village of Wantagh in 1867. At that time a railroad station was established there, but the name Jerusalem South created a great amount of confusion. This was because another station in the Bethpage area was known as Jerusalem or Jerusalem Station.[2] To end this seeming duplication of names, the western section of Jerusalem South adopted the name of Ridgewood and eventually its present name of Wantagh.

The eastern portion of Jerusalem South (which had also been known as Verity Town because of the many members of that family who lived there), held several meetings to choose a new name for its village. In January 1849, it was reported that, "The inhabitants of Jerusalem South and Seaman's Neck . . . have finally concluded that it shall be called 'Atlanticville.'"[3] This name was used for a number of years, although it never became official, and the post office retained Jerusalem South as its designation. Neither of these names was particularly acceptable to a majority of the area's residents, however, and finally they decided it was necessary to select a new name for the village.

For this reason a meeting of the area's residents was held, and the following notice (dated November 15, 1867) appeared in a local newspaper:

> At a meeting held in Atlanticville, known also by the P. O. name of Jerusalem South, Nov. 8th, 1867, for the purpose of changing the name of the village Post Office, it was unanimously resolved to call the village, the Village Station on the South Side Railroad, and the Post Office, Seaford. The first two changes to take place immediately, the latter as soon as the P. M. General consents thereto, at which time due notice will be given.[4]

The chairman of this meeting was Jacob Seaman Jackson Jones, who was familiarly known simply as Jackson Jones.[5] It is said that a valuable horse belonging to Jones had been stolen shortly before the meeting to choose a new name for the village was held. After a great deal of difficulty, the horse was found in Seaford, Delaware, and Jones went there to bring it back. With this incident firmly implanted in his mind, Jones supposedly suggested the name Seaford, which was accepted by the village residents.[6] Indirectly, therefore, the village of Seaford owes its name to a horse thief and also to the English town of Seaford, from which Seaford, Delaware, adopted its name.

Searingtown

Simon Searing was one of the original settlers of Hempstead, arriving there in 1644. He was also the founder of a family which eventually acquired substantial land holdings in Nassau County. Of his descendants, John Searing was the first to own land in the present-day Searingtown area, settling there in 1716.[1]

At the time John Searing purchased land there, the area was referred to as being near a place called Herricks. This locality continued to be called Herricks until the mid-1700s, when it was changed to Searingtown. By that time the Searing family was the principal landowner in the area. The first time the name Searingtown appeared in the Town Records was in a deed dated June 6, 1768.[2]

Although neighboring communities such as Albertson later absorbed part of the area known as Searingtown, this name has been in constant use since it was first adopted. It is also interesting to note that the Searing-Roslyn United Methodist Church, established in this area in 1785, was originally designated the Searingtown Methodist Episcopal Church, despite the fact that it is actually located in Herricks. The reason for this was that the first meeting was held in the house of Hannah Searing, and Coe Searing was one of the primary supporters of this church.[3]

South Floral Park

The history of the Village of South Floral Park was almost identical to that of Floral Park until it was decided to develop the area. In 1905, maps were filed with the Nassau County Clerk for the purpose of subdividing this property for a housing development.[1] The name selected by its promoters for the new village was Jamaica Square. That appellation was felt appropriate because the land was located on the road to Jamaica and adjacent to the village of Franklin Square.[2] It was also believed that a name which included the word Jamaica would attract people who thought they were settling near that village in Queens County.

This locality retained the name of Jamaica Square despite the fact that the original development was largely a failure. In November 1925, it was decided to incorporate the village and a local newspaper reported:

> Jamaica Square is the name of the newest incorporated village within the Town of Hempstead. Property owners of this community, which is located just east of Belmont Park, yesterday voted to incorporate. . . .
>
> Jamaica Square is a development featured by small lots and narrow streets. The people there feel that they can get better results from home government than through the township. Local improve-

ments are badly needed and because of various complications it was difficult for the town to provide what was demanded. With an assessed valuation of less than $100,000, however, the new village may find itself handicapped if an ambitious program is attempted.[3]

Despite the fact that this locality had become officially incorporated, little improvement was accomplished, and the Depression further hindered its development. In 1931, however, it was decided to change the name of the village because Jamaica Square was too often confused with Jamaica, Queens. At this time, therefore, the descriptive designation of its neighboring village to the north was partially adopted, and it was officially renamed South Floral Park.[4]

Stewart Manor

The area that is today the Village of Stewart Manor was for many years a portion of the common lands owned by the Town of Hempstead. Bordered on the north and west by Floral Park and New Hyde Park, and on the south by Franklin Square and Elmont, it remained unnamed until the twentieth century.

When Alexander T. Stewart purchased 7,170 acres of Hempstead's common lands in 1869, he became the owner of an area reaching from Floral Park to Bethpage, which included the section that was to become Stewart Manor. This locality remained undeveloped by Stewart, and after his death in 1876, it was held by his heirs until the early 1900s.[1] At that time this land was sold to William M. Brown, who proposed to develop the section. As Stewart Avenue, named after A. T. Stewart, was the main thoroughfare through the property, the area was named Stewart Manor in his honor.[2] The first use of this name appears on a real estate map dated 1907, which was filed in the Nassau County Clerk's office.

In 1914, Brown relinquished control of the area, and the following year a local newspaper announced his death as follows:

> William M. Brown, 64 years old, of Newcastle, Pa., who was elected to Congress in that district last November, and who was formerly Lieutenant Governor of Pennsylvania, died Sunday . . . after being ill a week with pneumonia. He was until last April the owner of a large amount of property near Garden City, known as the Stewart Manor, and which he gave in exchange for the entire block front on the east side of Madison Avenue, between Eighty-second and Eighty-third streets, Manhattan. More than $2,000,000 was involved in the transaction.[3]

This land had several subsequent owners, but in 1925, during a period of great real estate development, it was acquired by a firm known as Realty Associates, Inc. This group led by James Graham, built the first house there that year and began publicizing the place as Sunrise Gardens. The railroad station which had been built some years before, however, retained the name Stewart Manor.[4] Because that appellation was more attractive and distinctive than Sunrise Gardens, this village readopted its former name shortly before it became incorporated, on July 25, 1927.[5]

Syosset

The section that now comprises Syosset was originally a portion of a much larger area which generally was referred to as Cold Spring. At the annual Oyster Bay Town meeting held on April 3, 1821, it was "Voted, That Cold Spring district be divided and that the division line between the two districts be a Well in the road near Thomas West house." It was at that time, therefore, that the western section of the original district became known as the Little East Woods.[1]

The use of the name Little East Woods appeared in the Town Records until 1831, at which time it apparently ceased to be used. With the abandonment of the name Little East Woods, the area was then referred to in the Town Records as the "East District of Oysterbay." The first use of the name Syosset for this area appeared in the Town Records on May 23, 1846.[2]

It is interesting to note that the village of Oyster Bay had attempted to use the name of Syosset five months earlier. The Post Office Department consented to the use of the new name, and on January 20, 1846, the name of the Oyster Bay post office was changed to Syosset. The older residents of that village opposed this change so vigorously that the old name of Oyster Bay was restored after one week.[3]

William Wallace Tooker states that Syosset "is of Indian derivation: it has been evolved from the Dutch *Schouts,* 'a sheriff.' *Schout, Siocits, Syocits,* are some of the various stages of degradation, down to its present form."[4] Tooker rejects the suggestion that Syosset was the Indian name of the site of Oyster Bay village. This idea was apparently also believed by some of the residents of that village at the time the name of their post office was temporarily changed.[5]

Thomaston

Thomaston, like all the villages on the Great Neck peninsula, was originally referred to as a part of Madnans Neck. The name Madnans Neck first appears in the Town Records in a deed dated January 8, 1668. This neck of land or peninsula, like adjoining Cow Neck or Manhasset Neck, was used by the people of the town as a common pasture for their cattle. The designation of Great Neck in reference to this peninsula came into existence by 1672, and has been used to this day.[1] The Thomaston area, therefore, was also referred to as Great Neck, as were the other future villages in this locality.

In 1866, the North Shore Rail Road Company built a branch line to Great Neck and erected a station there. This station was originally known simply as Great Neck, but in November 1869, the name Brookdale came into use. It continued under that name until May 1872, when it reverted to Great Neck.[2] This entire area which is now known as Great Neck Plaza became the property of William R. Grace, later Mayor of New York City, in a most unusual manner. It is said, "that W. R. Grace was a rail passenger one day, and he had to use the washroom en route. Unfortunately, the washroom on the train was locked, which caused the future Mayor of New York considerable discomfort and embarrassment, and for which he successfully sued the railroad for $2,400. But the railroad happened to be broke even then and, in settlement, gave him all of what is now Great Neck Plaza, which he later subdivided."[3]

In 1859, Grace had married Lillian Gilchrist, and he named his newly acquired land near the Great Neck station, Thomaston in honor of her ancestral home in Maine.[4] Eventually that name was replaced by the more descriptive designation of Great Neck Plaza, by which name that village was incorporated in 1930.[5]

When the residents of the area to the southeast of Great Neck Plaza decided to incorporate as a village, it was necessary for them to first adopt a name. Because the Grace family continued to own large tracts of land in this section, the name Thomaston was again suggested and accepted by Hunter L. DeLatour, Henry A. Singley, Ernest A. Gallagher, and John W. Weight, the founders of the village. In October 1931, the Village of Thomaston was officially incorporated. No effort has been made to change the name since that time.[6]

Uniondale

The village of Uniondale was originally considered a part of that area which was known as East Meadow. After Hempstead was settled in 1644, the common lands to the east of the village were laid out as a pasture for the residents' cattle. The first reference to the designation of East Meadow appeared in the Town Records in an agreement dated April 10, 1658.[1]

The name East Meadow continued to be used for the entire area immediately east of Hempstead village until the 1770s. At that time the locality which bordered on the east edge of Hempstead adopted the name Turtle Hook. The Town Records first refer to this name in a deed dated March 13, 1779, from Hezekiah and Hannah Bedell to William Rushmore, which conveyed a house and property located at that place.[2]

Turtle Hook was used continuously as the name of this village until May 1853, when it was reported in a local newspaper that, "The old name of Turtle Hook, about a mile and a half east of the village of Hempstead, is about to be superceded by Union Dale."[3] This brief account was supplemented by a legal notice that appeared in another newspaper which stated that:

> At a meeting of the inhabitants of the neighborhood now called Turtle Hook, held at the school house in School District No. 2, town of Hempstead, for the purpose of giving a suitable name to the place; J. G. Martin was called to the Chair and J. S. Higbie appointed Secretary. It was unanimously

> Resolved, That as the name Turtle Hook is deemed unsuitable to the locality it be changed to and that it be hereafter called Union Dale.[4]

Unfortunately, no evidence has been found to indicate why the name of Uniondale was selected for this village. In May 1895, however, this appellation was approved by the postal authorities when the residents of the community applied for permission to establish a local post office there.[5]

In 1888, it had been noted that this place which "has been called Uniondale but in its waking it has taken to itself a new and more appropriate name East

Hempstead."[6] That designation, however, never became widely used, and Uniondale continued as the official name of the village.

There has been only one known attempt to change the name of this village, which has been known as Uniondale since 1853. This occurred in 1901, when a movement was begun to adopt Meadow Brook as its new designation. The Post Office Department, however, refused to approve this change because there was another post office in Orange County already using that designation.[7] When this attempt failed, it was suggested that another name be selected, but the majority of the area's residents preferred Uniondale, and it has been retained to this day.

University Gardens

University Gardens is one of the younger of Nassau County's villages, but for many years before attaining this status, it was generally regarded as the northern part of the Lake Success area. For this reason it was undoubtedly considered by the Matinecock Indians as being a portion of the locality they called Sacut. William Wallace Tooker stated that the name Sacut signifies, "'at the outlet,' . . . 'an outlet of a pond,' 'a stream flowing out of a pond or lake.'"[1]

Benjamin F. Thompson stated of the name Sacut that, "by a simple deflection in sound it might have been and probably was changed to Success." Tooker agreed with this theory as being the most likely reason for the adoption of the appellation of Success. The name Success first appeared in the Town Records in a deed dated September 22, 1679, referring to lands owned there by Richard Cornell.[2] This designation continued to be used from that time until the early 1800s.

The residents of this area decided to change its name in 1835. Again the nearby lake provided the new designation, as Lakeville was selected.[3] That name continued to be used until 1926, when the people residing south of the present village of University Gardens decided to incorporate their village. Before this happened, however, developments occurred which definitely separated the northern section from the future Village of Lake Success.

In the early 1920s, the area that was soon to become the Village of University Gardens was purchased by a group of men who proposed to build a golf course there. This land, which had previously been owned by Charles Hewlett, Charles Cornell, D. W. Bucklin, John Coughlin, and E. D. Morgan, consisted of 103 acres of land with a large frontage on Northern Boulevard.[4]

The purchase price of this land was said to have been $200,000. The group which acquired this property named it the University Golf Club. Either the venture was not successful or the value of the land became too great for it to be retained as a golf course, for it was offered for sale in the fall of 1925. Finally, in May 1926, a local newspaper reported that the property had been sold for $600,000. The purchasers of this former golf course were Louis H. Schwicke and George H. Higgins, representing the Athol Securities Corporation.[5]

It was said that this corporation intended to create a high class housing development there, and they adopted the name University Gardens. The first portion of this name was taken from the former golf course that had been located there and the second part from the development known as Russell Gardens, which was in the process of being built directly north of this village. By 1927, the name University Gardens was in use, and no attempts have been made to change this designation.[6]

Upper Brookville

The Village of Upper Brookville (like the Villages of Brookville and Old Brookville) was also a part of the area known by the Indians as Sucos or Suco's wigwam.[1] In referring to the name Sucos, William Wallace Tooker quotes W. W. Munsell's *History of Queens County* (1882) that, "Sucos: 'the site of the village of Brookville in the town of Oyster Bay, Queens Co., was called Suco's wigwam.'" Tooker states it is, "so called from *Suco,* the Indian who occupied the wigwam. His name is an abbreviation of *Suconamon,* from whom the land was purchased in the early days of the township."[2]

When Captain John Underhill was given a grant of land at this place by the Town of Oyster Bay in 1663, this eventually led to its name being changed to Wolverhampton. That designation, which first appeared in the Town Records in 1712, was probably given to the locality by the Underhill family in honor of their ancestral home.[3] In referring to this name, Henry C. Shelley stated of the Underhill family in England that, "it was in the southern region of the midland county of Staffordshire, and especially at Wolverhampton and its vicinity, that the most virile and prosperous Underhill family was seated."[4]

Wolverhampton had become changed to Wolver Hollow by 1768, and that designation continued to be used until the 1840s.[5] In February 1848, a local newspaper reported that the name of the area was to be changed from Wolver Hollow to Brookville.[6] No reason was given for this change, and it is unfortunate, therefore, that the derivation of the name Brookville has remained unknown.

Apparently this move was not viewed with favor by all of the residents of that area as a number of letters protesting the change appeared in a local newspaper.[7] Despite these protests the name Brookville was adopted and remained in use until various sections of the area began to incorporate as separate villages. In 1929, the Village of Old Brookville was incorporated, and in 1931, the Village of Brookville came into existence.

With the establishment of these villages, the northern section was excluded and, to preserve its independence, the residents there voted for incorporation, which became a reality on July 28, 1932. It was Mrs. C. Oliver Iselin, one of the village's original trustees, who suggested the name Upper Brookville because of its geographic location.[8]

Valley Stream

Prior to its settlement as a village, the northern portion of Valley Stream would have been considered as a part of Foster's Meadow, while the southern section would undoubtedly have been a part of the area known as Near Rockaway.

This area continued to be known by these names until Robert Pagan, an emigrant from Scotland, arrived and named it Valley Stream. That designation had come into use by the mid-1800s and was selected by Pagan, according to his grandson, because it described the small streams and valleys which ran through the place.[1] It was under the name Valley Stream that the residents of this village petitioned the Post Office Department in January 1870, for the right to establish a local post office.[2] In April of that year it was announced that:

> A new postoffice has been established at Valley Stream, Queens County, on that line of the South Side Railroad, and James Pagan has been appointed postmaster. Mr. Pagan is personally a good man, and in establishing an office at that point the P. O. Department has greatly accommodated a large and thriving community.[3]

It was also under the name of Valley Stream that this village was officially incorporated on February 14, 1925, and so this designation has been in constant use since it was first adopted in the mid-1800s.[4] Despite this fact, several colloquial names were used during the late 1800s and early 1900s, such as Hungry Harbor, Tigertown, and Cookie Hill.

The first of these areas, Hungry Harbor, was in the extreme southwest section of this village. It was so named because it was a squatters' settlement, and they went hungry a good part of the time.[5] Tigertown was located in the northeast part of the village. It was so named because of the drinking and fighting that took place there much of the time. In 1905, a local newspaper announced the end of that place by reporting that:

> The noted settlement of "Tigertown" with its dwellings built of old soap boxes and barrel staves is likely to be soon wiped off the map. The squatters who have held undisputed possession for about 25 years are up in arms. "Mayor Jake" Golder has held a council of war with his followers and says any invasion will be resisted to the last ditch. . . . However Messrs. John Miller and Christopher Schrieber who purchased that land—six acres—occupied by the "Tigers," at the county tax sale two years ago, have instructed their counsel to go ahead and get possession of the property as they have sold it under contract to P. A. Blake and must deliver it unencumbered. Consequently, notice in proceedings under the "squatters act" was served on Tuesday by Deputy Sheriff Meyers on Jacob Golder, Alonzo Johnson and George Johnson, reported owners of the shanties on the premises.[6]

The final of these colloquial names was Cookie Hill, an area in the northwest portion of the village. This was also a squatters' community and had a racy reputation, due to the fact that ladies of doubtful virtue, who have been recorded for posterity as "Black Sue," "Speckled Elsie," and others, lived there.[7]

Today the names North Valley Stream and South Valley Stream have come into use. Although they have no separate legal existence, they seem preferable to Cookie Hill, Hungry Harbor, and Tigertown.[8]

Wantagh

On April 7, 1838, it was announced that a new post office had been established to be known as Jerusalem South.[1] This appears to have been the first name given to the small settlement that was to become Wantagh, but unfortunately no mention is made as to why it was chosen.

Jerusalem South was used until the South Side Railroad of Long Island completed its line through the village in 1867. At that time a railroad station was established there, but the name Jerusalem South created a great deal of confusion. This was due to the fact that there was another railroad station in the Bethpage area known as Jerusalem or Jerusalem Station.[2]

To end the errors created by this seeming duplication of names, a meeting of the area's residents was held to consider the selection of a new name for the village. Many of the ladies present at the meeting were in favor of the name Yokohama, but this was "considered as being too ponderous." James M. Seaman then suggested the name of Ridgewood, and it was unanimously adopted by those present.[3] The postal authorities accepted the new designation, and the name of the post office was officially changed in November 1868.[4] In Queens County, however, another village also became known as Ridgewood. This created the same confusion that had existed when the old name of Jerusalem South had been in use.[5]

For this reason another public meeting was held on May 29, 1891, at the home of J. A. Seymour. At this time a resolution was offered by the Village Improvement Association, suggesting that the name of the village be changed to avoid future confusion. At least one person, Counselor A. W. Seaman, was opposed to changing the name of Ridgewood. He stated, "a change would require a number of years to receive necessary publicity to enable all of one's relatives and business acquaintances to become familiar with same."[6] The majority of the persons present, however, were in favor of the resolution.

To prevent any further duplication, it was decided to select an Indian name, and the name of Wyandance, chief of the Montauketts, was suggested by Thomas B. Seaman.[7] In 1657, Wantagh had signed the deed confirming the original sale of the lands comprising the Town of Hempstead.[8] Wantagh was a variation of the name Wyandance, and this was their final selection. According to William Wallace Tooker, Wantagh or "*Wyandance* is derived from *waian-* or *wayan=wauontam,* [meaning] (he is) wise . . . or 'the wise speaker or talker.'"[9]

The Post Office Department approved this new name and put it into effect on July 1, 1891.[10] The Long Island Rail Road began using Wantagh as the name of their station on October 1, 1891.[11] The section immediately north of the village of Wantagh has been referred to as North Wantagh since the early 1900s. According to postal authorities, however, North Wantagh has never been recognized as the official designation of that area.[12]

Westbury

The present-day Village of Westbury actually adopted its name from the Village of Old Westbury. In 1675, Henry Willis purchased land in the Old Westbury area from Captain John Seaman. The name Westbury was given to this section by Willis, after a town in his native County of Wiltshire, England.[1]

The name Westbury was in use as early as 1683, and while it was primarily the designation of today's Old Westbury, it was also used in referring to the area south of that village.[2] When the then village of Westbury attempted to establish a post office in 1841, they learned that this appellation was already being used by a village in Cayuga County.[3] For this reason, the name of the town was selected, and their post office was known as North Hempstead from 1841 to 1868.[4]

Despite the fact that their post office was known as North Hempstead, this locality never gave up the name Westbury. Finally, the residents decided that too much confusion was being caused by having a postal designation that was different than the village name. For this reason they requested the right to change the name of the post office and village to Old Westbury. This request was granted, and Old Westbury became the official name of that village in April 1868.[5]

The present Village of Westbury, which is located to the south of Old Westbury, began to be developed in the 1870s and 1880s. Although the entire area had been generally known as Westbury, this section, like Old Westbury, was forced to adopt a new name when the residents applied to establish a post office. The postal authorities accepted Westbury Station as its new designation, and the post office there opened in March 1882. The reason that name was selected was because the Long Island Rail Road had established a station there in the 1860s.[6]

Westbury Station continued to be used as the post office designation until December 1908, when it was changed to Westbury. This was possible because the upstate village was no longer using that name. Westbury then became the name of this village, and it was incorporated under this name in 1932.[8]

Near Westbury and Westbury South are areas in the neighboring Town of Hempstead which took their names from the Village of Westbury. Neither of these localities, however, has any official village status.

West Hempstead

The locality which is now known as the village of West Hempstead was originally referred to simply as Hempstead or near Hempstead. When that village was incorporated, however, this area was not included within its bounds. Thereafter it was generally referred to as west of Hempstead.

The actual name West Hempstead came into existence when the Long Island Rail Road constructed a station on its branch line at that place in 1893. They named this station West Hempstead, and the station which was constructed a short distance to the south was named Hempstead Gardens. The population of these areas did not warrant the construction of two stations. However they were built because Austin Corbin, president of the railroad, had extensive land holdings there which he was attempting to promote.[1]

Gradually the village of West Hempstead began to grow and now includes most of the area that was then known as Hempstead Gardens, in addition to a portion of the locality known as Munson.[2] On September 12, 1949, the Hempstead Post Office established an annex in West Hempstead, and in March 1962, the present West Hempstead Branch Post Office came into existence.[3]

Williston Park

The history of the Village of Williston Park was identical to that of the Village of East Williston, until 1926. Like East Williston, it had acquired its name from the Willis family.[1] Henry Willis, who settled in the Old Westbury area in 1675, was the first member of this family to reside in present-day Nassau County.[2]

Later generations of the Willis family moved to the locality of the present-day villages of Williston Park and East Williston. This area was then known simply as Williston and continued to be referred to by that name until 1879, when the residents attempted to establish a post office. At that time it became necessary to change the designation of this village to East Williston, because there was already a post office in Erie County that was using the name Williston.[3]

From 1879 until 1926, this area was known as East Williston. In 1926, however, the locality was divided into two incorporated villages, with the eastern section retaining the name East Williston and the western section adopting the name Williston Park.[4] The dividing line between these villages is the railroad line running north to Glen Cove. According to Vincent Seyfried, there was a stop at East Williston as early as 1880, and the station serving these villages was probably built about 1887. The post office serving this locality was opened at East Williston on May 19, 1879, and transferred to Williston Park in 1958, as that village had the larger population.[5]

In addition to being the first family to settle in the locality, the Willis family provided the area with two of its most illustrious residents, both of whom were born in the Williston Park section: Henry M. Willis, who invented the world famous East Williston Road Cart; and Eugene V. Willis, who became Supervisor of the Town of North Hempstead.[6] This is possibly the reason why there have been no known attempts to change the names of these villages since they were incorporated.

Woodbury

On June 2, 1697, Edward White, Thomas Townsend, and John Williams purchased a large tract of land in the eastern section of the Town of Oyster Bay from Wee Asher Wamehas, sachem of Sequatague. By 1745, various sections within this area began to assume separate identities and names. The section which was to eventually become the village of Woodbury was then given the name of

East Woods. This apparently descriptive designation first appeared in the Town Records in a deed dated September 11, 1746.[1]

By 1836, the village of East Woods had become sufficiently populous for its residents to request that the Post Office Department establish a local branch office there.[2] This request was approved, but the name East Woods does not appear to have been acceptable to the postal authorities. Possibly the reason for this was that the present village of Syosset was known as Little East Woods at that time, and it was feared that this name would cause confusion.[3]

In August 1836, therefore, a local newspaper reported, "A new post-office has been established and named Woodbury, in Queens County, Long Island, N.Y., and John V. Hewlett appointed post-master."[4] This appears to have been the first mention of the name Woodbury. Unfortunately, no reason was given as to why this appellation was selected.

Although the name Woodbury was adopted at that time, and has remained in use to the present day, the post office, which had established the name, did not prove to be permanent. In April 1840, that office was transferred to West Hills, in Suffolk County.

Then, in May 1858, it was reported that, "A new Post Office has been established in the village of Woodbury, in this county, and John J. Whiting appointed Post Master."[5] This post office has apparently been in continuous existence since that time. There have been no known attempts to change either its name or the name of this village.

Woodmere

Originally the locality that was to become the villages of Woodmere and Woodsburgh was a part of that large geographical area which was known as Near Rockaway. Samuel Wood purchased this land in 1869, and gave it the designation of Woodsburgh to perpetuate his family name.[1] The manner in which this village was developed was graphically described in a booklet published in 1871:

> Before this century began, four brothers named Wood were born and raised in the vicinity of what is henceforth to be known as Woodsburgh. In time they removed to New York City and established themselves in the wholesale liquor trade, on Fulton Street. . . . One by one, three of the brothers died, and, being bachelors, left their respective fortunes to the survivors, and finally to the sole survivor and present representative of the family, Samuel Wood, now seventy-six years of age. He is infirm physically; mentally, he is as bright as he ever was. He conceived the notion of spending a portion of his large fortune in improving the place of his birth. To this end he bought, in successive parcels, the property now known as Woodsburgh, with the intention of making it a fashionable summer resort. Being a native of the village of Rockaway, and familiar with the locality, he chose the present site upon which to erect his improvements, and, as he expresses it, to lay the foundation of a town he hopes will grow and prosper through all time.[2]

After Samuel Wood died in 1878, this property came into the possession of Abraham Hewlett and the Woodmere Land Improvement Company, who continued its development.[3] During the ensuing years the population of this area increased sufficiently for it to feel the necessity of having a post office. The residents of Woodsburgh, therefore, applied to the postal authorities for permission to establish a local branch office. This request was granted, but only on the condition that the name of the village first be changed. The reason the Post Office Department demanded this change of name was that they felt Woodsburgh was too similar to the name Woodbury and would create confusion.[4]

Therefore, in October 1897, the name of this village was changed to Woodmere and this designation has been used since that time.[5] The only known attempt to alter the name of this village occurred in the early 1890s. At that time the Long Island Rail Road renamed its station there Glenhurst.[6] This appellation was not accepted by the residents of the village, however, and the name of the area's developer was soon re-adopted.[7]

Woodsburgh

The history of the incorporated Village of Woodsburgh was identical to that of present-day Woodmere until 1912. This locality was a part of the area originally known as Near Rockaway and was also a part of the land purchased by Samuel Wood in 1869.[1] The entire area owned by Wood became known as Woodsburgh and continued under that name until 1897.

At that time the residents of the area were forced to change the designation of their village in order to receive permission to establish a local post office.[2] For this reason the entire locality became known as Woodmere and that name has been in use to this day.

The residents of the southern portion of the village of Woodmere, however, decided to separate from the remainder of Wood's original development and become an incorporated village. This was accomplished on November 14, 1912, but before that was possible, it was necessary to select a name for their new village.[3] For this reason the name Woodsburgh was re-adopted and in this way, the original appellation given to the area by Samuel Wood has been preserved. Since this village was incorporated in 1912, no known attempts have been made to change its designation.

Epilogue

The most appropriate way to conclude this work is to quote what historian Benjamin F. Thompson wrote more than 150 years ago:

> We cannot help expressing our sincere regret at the disposition so prevalent in the present day, for changing the name of places; many of those adopted being remarkable for little else than their singularity and inappropriateness. From a historical and economical viewpoint, this passion for change is much to be lamented, as leading in the end to confusion and uncertainty. Old names, like old friends, should not be changed for light and transient causes, much less from mere whim and caprice; the consequences of change may at a future period be attended with more serious evils than are now contemplated, by those concerned in this useless not to say mischievous, innovation.[1]

Appendix

Population of Nassau County Communities

Village	1990 Population	Est. 1998 Population	Area in Sq. Miles	Pop. Density Per Sq. Mile
Albertson	5,166	5,186	0.7	7,409
Atlantic Beach (v)	1,933	1,957	0.5	3,914
Baldwin	22,719	22,633	2.9	7,804
Baldwin Harbor	7,899	7,996	1.2	6,663
Barnum Island	2,624	2,645	0.9	2,939
Baxter Estates (v)	961	988	0.2	4,940
Bay Park	2,280	2,276	0.5	4,552
Bayville (v)	7,193	7,187	1.4	5,134
Bellerose (v)	1,101	1,079	0.1	10,790
Bellerose Terrace	2,014	2,076	0.1	20,760
Bellmore	16,438	16,132	2.5	6,453
Bethpage	15,761	16,283	3.6	4,523
Brookville (v)	3,716	3,430	4.0	858
Carle Place	5,107	5,059	0.9	5,621
Cedarhurst (v)	5,716	5,850	0.7	8,357
Centre Island (v)	439	453	1.1	412
Cove Neck (v)	332	334	1.3	257
East Atlantic Beach	2,168	2,317	0.7	3,310
East Garden City	4,583	4,440	3.1	1,432
East Hills (v)	6,746	6,692	2.3	2,910
East Massapequa	19,550	19,409	3.5	5,545
East Meadow	36,909	37,262	6.3	5,915
East Norwich	2,698	2,717	1.0	2,717
East Rockaway (v)	10,152	10,131	1.0	10,131
East Williston (v)	2,515	2,477	0.6	4,128
Elmont	28,612	28,807	3.4	8,473
Farmingdale (v)	8,022	8,214	1.1	7,467
Floral Park (v)	16,063	16,104	1.4	11,503
Flower Hill (v)	4,490	4,478	1.6	2,799
Franklin Square	28,205	28,233	2.9	9,736
Freeport (v)	39,894	40,238	4.6	8,747
Garden City (v)	21,675	20,775	5.3	3,920
Garden City Park	7,437	7,469	1.0	7,469
Garden City South	4,073	4,041	0.4	10,103
Glen Cove, City of	24,149	24,546	6.6	3,719
Glen Head	4,488	4,523	1.6	2,827
Glenwood Landing	3,424	3,448	1.0	3,448
Great Neck (v)	8,745	8,894	1.3	6,842

Village	1990 Population	Est. 1998 Population	Area in Sq. Miles	Pop. Density Per Sq. Mile
Great Neck Estates (v)	2,790	2,826	0.8	3,533
Great Neck Gardens	1,516	1,585	0.2	7,925
Great Neck Plaza (v)	5,897	5,994	0.3	19,980
Greenvale	965	929	4.7	198
Harbor Hills	694	716	0.1	7,160
Harbor Isle	1,373	1,318	n.a.	n.a.
Hempstead (v)	49,453	47,250	3.7	12,770
Herricks	4,097	4,003	0.6	6,672
Hewlett	6,620	6,575	0.9	7,306
Hewlett Bay Park (v)	440	429	0.4	1,073
Hewlett Harbor (v)	1,193	1,158	0.7	1,654
Hewlett Neck (v)	547	539	0.2	2,695
Hicksville	40,174	39,811	6.8	5,855
Inwood	7,767	7,631	1.6	4,769
Island Park (v)	4,860	4,927	0.4	12,318
Jericho	13,141	13,171	4.0	3,293
Kensington (v)	1,104	1,086	0.3	3,620
Kings Point (v)	4,843	4,772	3.3	1,446
Lake Success (v)	2,484	2,482	1.8	1,379
Lakeview	5,476	5,578	1.0	5,578
Lattingtown (v)	1,859	1,891	3.8	498
Laurel Hollow (v)	1,748	1,775	2.9	612
Lawrence (v)	6,513	6,540	3.8	1,721
Levittown	53,286	52,601	6.9	7,623
Lido Beach	2,786	2,736	1.7	1,609
Locust Valley	3,963	3,930	1.0	3,930
Long Beach, City of	33,510	35,030	2.1	16,681
Lynbrook (v)	19,208	19,525	2.0	9,763
Malverne (v)	9,054	9,017	1.1	8,197
Malverne Park Oaks	488	485	0.1	4,850
Manhasset	7,718	7,773	2.4	3,239
Manhasset Hills	3,722	3,665	0.6	6,108
Manorhaven (v)	5,672	5,843	0.5	11,686
Massapequa	22,018	21,801	3.6	6,056
Massapequa Park (v)	18,044	17,817	2.2	8,099
Matinecock (v)	872	891	2.6	343
Merrick	23,042	22,811	4.2	5,431
Mill Neck (v)	977	986	2.6	379
Mineola (v)	18,994	19,052	1.9	10,027
Munsey Park (v)	2,692	2,693	0.5	5,386
Muttontown (v)	3,024	3,155	6.1	517
New Cassel	10,257	10,618	1.5	7,079
New Hyde Park (v)	9,728	9,708	0.9	10,787

Village	1990 Population	Est. 1998 Population	Area in Sq. Miles	Pop. Density Per Sq. Mile
North Bellmore	19,707	19,782	2.6	7,608
North Hills (v)	3,453	3,962	2.8	1,415
North Lynbrook	689	712	0.1	7,120
North Massapequa	19,365	19,230	3.0	6,410
North Merrick	12,113	12,042	1.8	6,690
North New Hyde Pk.	14,359	14,203	2.0	7,102
North Valley Stream	14,574	14,876	1.9	7,829
North Wantagh	12,276	11,994	1.9	6,313
Oceanside	32,423	32,542	5.0	6,508
Old Bethpage	5,610	5,435	4.1	1,326
Old Brookville (v)	1,823	1,947	4.0	487
Old Westbury (v)	3,897	3,923	8.5	462
Oyster Bay	6,687	6,587	1.2	5,489
Oyster Bay Cove (v)	2,109	2,270	4.2	540
Plainedge	8,739	8,573	1.4	6,124
Plainview	26,207	25,508	5.7	4,475
Plandome (v)	1,347	1,340	0.5	2,680
Plandome Heights (v)	852	841	0.2	4,205
Plandome Manor (v)	790	773	0.5	1,546
Point Lookout	1,519	1,515	10.9	139
Port Washington	15,387	15,614	4.2	3,718
Port Washington North (v)	2,736	2,708	0.5	5,416
Rockville Centre (v)	24,727	24,659	3.3	7,472
Roosevelt	15,030	15,044	1.8	8,358
Roslyn (v)	1,965	2,032	0.6	3,387
Roslyn Estates (v)	1,184	1,166	0.4	2,915
Roslyn Harbor (v)	1,114	1,096	1.2	913
Roslyn Heights	6,405	6,466	1.5	4,311
Russell Gardens (v)	1,027	1,027	0.2	5,135
Saddle Rock (v)	832	823	0.2	4,115
Saddle Rock Estates	294	305	0.1	3,050
Salisbury	12,226	12,162	1.7	7,154
Sands Point (v)	2,477	2,481	4.2	591
Sea Cliff (v)	5,054	5,077	1.1	4,615
Seaford	15,597	15,718	2.6	6,045
Searingtown	5,020	4,925	0.9	5,472
South Farmingdale	15,377	15,105	2.2	6,866
South Floral Park (v)	1,478	1,487	0.1	14,870
South Hempstead	3,014	2,975	0.6	492
South Valley Stream	5,328	5,297	0.9	5,886
Stewart Manor (v)	2,002	1,950	0.2	9,750
Syosset	18,967	18,742	5.0	3,748
Thomaston (v)	2,612	2,575	0.4	6,438

Village	1990 Population	Est. 1998 Population	Area in Sq. Miles	Pop. Density Per Sq. Mile
Uniondale	20,328	20,755	2.7	7,687
University Gardens	4,419	4,391	0.6	7,318
Upper Brookville (v)	1,453	1,586	4.3	369
Valley Stream (v)	33,946	33,930	3.4	9,979
Wantagh	18,567	18,826	3.8	4,954
West Hempstead	17,689	17,714	2.7	6,561
Westbury (v)	13,060	13,387	2.5	5,355
Williston Park (v)	7,516	7,494	0.6	12,490
Woodbury	8,008	8,472	5.0	1,694
Woodmere	15,578	15,388	2.6	5,918
Woodsburgh (v)	1,190	1,221	0.4	3,053
Nassau County Total	1,287,348	1,290,557	286.8	4,500

v = Incorporated Village
n.a. = not available

Note: East Garden City includes population in the Hofstra residence halls; this is also true of other communities with college dormitories, i.e., Garden City (Adelphi), Kings Point (U. S. Merchant Marine Academy), and Brookville (C.W. Post). The East Meadow population includes those in the Nassau County Jail, and Uniondale figures include those in the A. Holly Patterson Geriatric Center.

In terms of land area, Nassau with 288 square miles is four times the size of Kings or Brooklyn (70 square miles), two-and-one-half times the size of Queens (109 square miles), and less than one-third the size of Suffolk County (911 square miles); Long Island's total is 1,378 square miles and the total area including water is considerably higher—1,723 square miles. Brooklyn's population in 1990 was 2.3 million, Queens, 2.0 million, and Suffolk, 1.3 million. The population in Suffolk County is still increasing, while Nassau's peaked at 1.4 million in 1970 and has been at a relatively stable level since the mid-1980s.

Sources: 1990 population and area from *1990 Census of Population, New York* (Washington, DC: Bureau of the Census, 1991), CPH-2-34, Table 8, pp. 22-24; estimated 1998 population from Long Island Power Authority (LIPA), *Population Survey 1998* (Uniondale: LIPA, 1998), pp. 7-12; population density calculated using 1998 estimates of population and land area.

Notes

Foreword

1. Natalie A. Naylor, "Introduction," to *Evoking a Sense of Place,* edited by Joann P. Krieg (Interlaken, NY: Heart of the Lakes Publishing,1988), p. 17; see also Thomas J. Schlereth "Local History as Universal History," in *Evoking a Sense of Place*, pp. 19-27.

2. George R. Stewart, *Names on the Land: A Historical Account of Place-Naming in the United States,* 2d ed. (Boston: Houghton-Mifflin, 1967); George R. Stewart, *American Place-Names: A Concise and Selective Dictionary for the Continental United States of America* (New York: Oxford University Press, 1970); Karl H. Proehl and Barbara Shupe, *Long Island Gazetteer: A Guide to Current and Historical Place Names* (Bayside: LDA Publishers, 1984); Doris Nostrand, "Pronunciation, Geographical, and Historical Dictionary of Selected Place Names of Suffolk County, New York" (M.S. report, C. W. Post Library School, 1971); and William Mulvihill, *South Fork Place Names* (Sag Harbor: Brickiln Press, 1995). The *Long Island Gazetteer* is particularly useful for references on early maps.

3. Richard Winsche, "History of the Place Names of Nassau County's Villages," M.A. thesis, Graduate Faculties of Long Island University (C. W. Post College), 1968. A copy is in the Nassau County Museum collection of the Long Island Studies Institute at Hofstra University (917.4721 W). The dissertation includes a chapter on the methodology of place-name research which briefly discusses methods used by English and American historians (pp. 5-17). The author chose not to include that material in this published version.

4. The Nassau County Museum collection in the Long Island Studies Institute at Hofstra University has microfilms of these and other Long Island newspapers.

5. See John A. Strong, *The Algonquian Peoples of Long Island From Earliest Times to 1700* (Interlaken, NY: Empire State Books, 1997), pp. 26-27; and Gaynell Stone Levine and Nancy Bonvillain, eds., *Languages and Lore of the Long Island Indians,* vol. 4 in *Readings in Long Island Archaeology and Ethnohistory* (Stony Brook: Suffolk County Archaeological Association, 1980), pp. 1-192.

6. Some other hints to deciphering colonial writing: i and j and u and v were often used interchangeably; y was also used for th (as in ye, pronounced the). A useful guide for deciphering manuscripts is Harriet Stryker-Rodda, *Understanding Colonial Handwriting,* reprinted from *New Jersey History* (Newark: New Jersey Historical Society, 1980).

7. On the formation of Nassau County, see Edward J. Smits, "Creating a New County: Nassau," *Long Island Historical Journal* 11 (Spring 1999): 129-44; Natalie A. Naylor, "The Formation of Nassau County," *Nassau County Historical Society Journal* 53 (1998): 8-10; and Geoffrey Mohan, "Nassau's Difficult Birth," in *Long Island: Our Story,* by Newsday (Melville: Newsday, 1998), pp. 232-35.

8. Communities also are sometimes popularly referred to as "towns," as in Allen Oren, *This Old Town,* 12 videocassettes (Woodbury: News 12, Long Island, 1993), and Newsday, *Home Town: Long Island* (Melville: Newsday, 1999).

9. Prior to 1910, state law required a minimum population of 250. Roswell Eldredge who wanted to incorporate his estate had the law changed to a minimum population of fifty. This enabled him to incorporate the Village of Saddle Rock since his own family and those of his employees who resided on his estate numbered more than fifty. The 1932 state law also required a *maximum* area of three square miles for new villages to ensure a density of population. It did not prevent existing villages from expanding their

boundaries and annex contiguous territory which themselves might not qualify to become new incorporated villages. Brookville, Laurel Hollow, and Muttontown were among the villages which extended their local control to neighboring areas in the 1950s. See Dennis P. Sobin, *Dynamics of Community Change: The Case of Long Island's Declining "Gold Coast"* (Port Washington: Ira J. Friedman, 1968), pp. 99-103, 107-9; *Laws of the State of New York, 1910* (Albany: J. B. Lyon Co., 1910), 1:461. Current requirements are a minimum of 500 people and a maximum area of five square miles.

10. A listing of historical societies can be found in Joann P. Krieg and Natalie A. Naylor, *To Know the Place: Exploring Long Island History,* rev. ed. (Interlaken, NY: Heart of the Lakes Publishing, 1995), pp. 139-43. *To Know the Place* also includes "An Introduction to Resources for Exploring Local History," pp. 75-82, and extensive bibliographies, pp. 83-128.

11. A convenient listing of Long Island population for earlier years is in Long Island Regional Planning Board, *Historical Population of Long Island Communities, 1790-1980* (Hauppauge: Long Island Regional Planning Board, 1982).

Introduction

1. William M. Beauchamp, *Aboriginal Place-Names of New York* (Albany: New York State Education Department, 1906); James Ellsworth DeKay, *Indian Names of Long Island Localities* (Oyster Bay: William L. Swan, 1920); and William Wallace Tooker, *The Indian Place-Names of Long Island and Islands Adjacent, With Their Probable Significations* (New York: G. P. Putnam's Sons, 1911). Tooker's book was reprinted in 1962 by I. J. Friedman in Port Washington.

2. Donald Dean Parker, *Local History; How to Gather It, Write It, and Publish It* (New York: Social Science Research Council, 1944), p. 37.

3. Hagstrom Map Company, *Hagstrom Nassau County Atlas* (Maspeth: Hagstrom Map Company, 1992); Long Island Association, *Long Island, The Sunrise Homeland, 1957,* 18th ed. (Garden City: Long Island Association, 1957); Nassau County Planning Commission, *Nassau County, New York, Data Book* (Mineola: Nassau County Planning Commission, 1985); and Proehl and Shupe, *Long Island Gazetteer.*

Albertson

1. Benjamin D. Hicks, ed., *Records of the Towns of North and South Hempstead, Long Island, N.Y.,* 8 vols. (Jamaica: Long Island Farmer Print, 1896-1904), 2:31. Hereafter cited as Hicks, *Hempstead Town Records.*

2. W. W. Munsell, *History of Queens County, New York, With Illustrations, Portraits, and Sketches of Prominent Families and Individuals* (New York: W. W. Munsell Company, 1882), p. 430.

3. Queens County Deeds, Liber 69, p. 284 (microfilm in Nassau County Museum collection, Long Island Studies Institute at Hofstra University).

4. Vincent F. Seyfried, *The Long Island Rail Road, A Comprehensive History,* 7 vols. (Garden City: Vincent F. Seyfried, 1966), 3:15.

5. Queens County Deeds, Liber 451, p. 495.

6. *Nassau Daily Review-Star,* October 8, 1952; *New York Herald Tribune,* April 18, 1965.

7. Seyfried, *Long Island Rail Road,* 3:203.

Atlantic Beach

1. *South Side Observer,* February 1, 1889.

2. Henry Isham Hazelton, *The Boroughs of Brooklyn and Queens, Counties of Nassau and Suffolk, Long Island, New York, 1609-1924,* 7 vols. (New York: Lewis

Historical Publishing Company, 1925), 5:8. Hereafter cited as Hazelton, *Boroughs of Brooklyn and Queens.*

 3. Ibid., 5:8.

 4. Ibid., 5:8.

 5. *Nassau Daily Review,* February 23, 1926.

 6. Letter from Atlantic Beach Village Clerk John F. Duncombe to the author, August 12, 1964. This and other letters from village clerks are on deposit in the Nassau County Museum collection at the Long Island Studies Institute, Hofstra University.

Baldwin

 1. Hicks, *Hempstead Town Records,* 1:278.

 2. Writers' Program of the Works Projects Administration [WPA], *Hick's Neck, The Story of Baldwin, Long Island* (Baldwin: Baldwin National Bank & Trust Company, 1939, p. 15. Hereafter cited as WPA, *Hick's Neck.*

 3. Ibid., pp. 19, 23.

 4. Ibid., pp. 23, 31, 33.

 5. *Picket,* July 10, 1868; Seyfried, *Long Island Rail Road,* 1:77. (The *Picket,* published in Rockville Centre from 1865-1870, became the *South Side Observer* in 1870.)

 6. *Picket,* July 10, 1868, July 17, 1868.

 7. Seyfried, *Long Island Rail Road,* 1:77.

 8. WPA, *Hick's Neck,* p. 33.

 9. Seyfried, *Long Island Rail Road,* 1:77.

 10. *South Side Observer,* January 22, 1892, January 29, 1892.

 11. Ibid., May 13, 1892; *East Norwich Enterprise,* August 31, 1895.

 12. *South Side Observer,* June 11, 1897, November 23, 1900.

 13. *Daily Review,* December 18, 1925.

 14. On the history of Baldwin, see Glenn F. Sitterly, *The Illustrated Story of Baldwin, Long Island, N. Y. Through the Years* (Baldwin: Baldwin Union Free School District, 1984).

Baxter Estates

 1. Hicks, *Hempstead Town Records,* 1:263.

 2. *Hempstead Inquirer,* July 30, 1859.

 3. Hicks, *Hempstead Town Records,* 3:327; and Hazelton, *Boroughs of Brooklyn and Queens,* 5:98.

 4. Ibid., 5:98, 118.

 5. *Port Washington News,* May 21, 1910.

 6. E. Belcher Hyde, *Atlas of Nassau County, Long Island, N.Y.* (New York: E. Belcher Hyde, 1914), p. 3.

 7. Letter from Charles Hyde Walker to the author, May 18, 1967.

Bay Park

 1. 1912 Tax Roll, Village of East Rockaway, Long Island, p. 26.

 2. Ibid., pp. 17-18.

 3. *1942-1943 Year Book of the Bay Park Property Owners' Association, Inc.,* p. 16.

 4. Ibid., pp. 13, 16.

 5. Ibid., p. 16.

Bayville

1. John Cox, Jr., ed., *Oyster Bay Town Records,* 8 vols. (New York: Tobias A. Wright, 1916-1940) 1:11.

2. Ibid., 1:354.

3. Ibid., 1:202.

4. Ibid., 5:690-91.

5. *Glen Cove Gazette,* June 25, 1859.

6. *South Side Observer,* February 11, 1881.

7. On the history of Bayville, see Carleton Upright, *The Times and Tides of Bayville, Long Island, N. Y.* (Bayville: Privately printed, 1969).

Bellerose

1. Letter from Bellerose Village Clerk Otto A. Philipp to the author, August 18, 1964.

2. Ibid.

3. Ibid.

4. *Long Island Democrat,* August 23, 1898.

5. Queens County Deeds, Liber 971, p. 395.

6. *Long Island Democrat,* March 21, 1893.

7. Long Island Rail Road, *Timetable,* October 1898.

8. Letter from Bellerose Village Clerk Otto A. Philipp to the author, August 18, 1964.

On the history of Bellerose, see Village of Bellerose 50th Anniversary Committee, *Village of Bellerose 50th Anniversary Commemorative Album* (Bellerose: Village of Bellerose, 1974).

Bellerose Terrace

1. Lucius H. Hallock, *A Hallock Genealogy* (Orient: Lucius H. Hallock, 1926), p. 253.

2. *Queens County Sentinel,* August 12, 1886.

3. E. Belcher Hyde, *Real Estate Map of Nassau County, Long Island, N.Y.* (New York: E. Belcher Hyde, 1923), p. 3.

4. Nassau County Deeds, Liber 3593, p. 475 (microfilm in Nassau County Museum collection, Long Island Studies Institute at Hofstra University).

5. *Gateway,* March 16, 1939.

Bellmore

1. Hicks, *Hempstead Town Records,* 1:322.

2. Munsell, *History of Queens County,* p. 169; and Nathaniel S. Prime, *A History of Long Island, From Its First Settlement by Europeans, to the Year 1845, With Special Reference to its Ecclesiastical Concerns* (New York: Robert Carter, 1845), p. 291.

3. *Hempstead Inquirer,* December 18, 1858.

4. Ibid., December 25, 1858.

5. Seyfried, *Long Island Rail Road,* 1:78.

6. F. W. Beers, *Atlas of Long Island* (New York: Beers, Comstock & Cline, 1873), p. 120.

7. On the history of Bellmore, see Kenneth M. Foreman, *A Profile of the Bellmores, With Historical Commentary and Background Information* (Bellmore: Bellmore Life and the Historical Society of the Bellmores, 1994).

Bethpage

1. Iris Gibbs and Alonzo Gibbs, *Bethpage Bygones* (Bethpage: Kinsman Press, 1962), p. 8. Hereafter cited as Gibbs, *Bethpage Bygones.*

2. Mildred H. Smith, *Early History of the Long Island Railroad 1834-1900* (Uniondale: Salisbury Printers, 1958), p. 7.

3. *Picket,* March 29, 1867.

4. *South Side Observer,* November 21, 1890.

5. Ibid., November 21, 1890, September 11, 1891.

6. *Nassau Daily Review,* April 14, 1936.

7. Gibbs, *Bethpage Bygones,* pp. 47-49.

8. *Nassau Daily Review,* April 14, 1936.

9. Gibbs, *Bethpage Bygones,* p. 49.

10. *Nassau Daily Review,* October 1, 1936.

11. On the history of Bethpage, see also [Harrison deF] Terry/Terence S. [*sic*] Hunt, *Bethpage: The Years of Development, 1840-1910* (East Farmingdale: Oakdale Press, 1973, 1976); and Iris Gibbs and Alonzo Gibbs, *Harking Back* (Waldeboro, ME: Kinsman Publications, 1984).

Brookville

1. Cox, *Oyster Bay Town Records,* 1:79.

2. Tooker, *Indian Place-Names,* pp. 250-51.

3. Cox, *Oyster Bay Town Records,* 1:7, 3:503.

4. Henry C. Shelley, *John Underhill Captain of New England and New Netherland* (New York: D. Appleton and Company, 1932), p. 1.

5. Cox, *Oyster Bay Town Records,* 4:674.

6. *Long Island Democrat,* January 25, 1848.

7. *Long Island Farmer,* February 29, 1948, March 7, 1948.

Carle Place

1. Norma I. Ehlen, *This is Carle Place* (Carle Place: Carle Place Chamber of Commerce, 1958), p. 4.

2. Hicks, *Hempstead Town Records,* 7:155.

3. Ehlen, *This Is Carle Place,* pp. 4, 9.

4. *Long Island Democrat,* June 28, 1837.

5. Ehlen, *This Is Carle Place,* p. 9.

6. Hyde, *Atlas of Nassau County,* 1914, p. 3.

7. Ehlen, *This Is Carle Place,* pp. 9, 10.

8. *Long Island Democrat,* June 28, 1837.

9. Ehlen, *This Is Carle Place,* p. 10.

Cedarhurst

1. Seyfried, *Long Island Rail Road,* 1:23-25, 80.

2. *Picket,* February 25, 1870.

3. *South Side Observer,* April 22, 1887.

4. Ibid., March 21, 1890.

5. Letter from Cedarhurst Village Clerk Edmund M. Greenwald to the author, August 12, 1964.

On the history of the Five Towns, including Cedarhurst, see:

> Deschin, Celia Spalter. "A Community Self-Portrait: The Five Towns as Seen Through the Eyes of Its Adult Residents, Its Adolescents, Health and Welfare Experts, and Its Community Leaders." Typescript, 1965.

Copy in Nassau County Museum collection, Long Island Studies Institute at Hofstra University.

Our Towns, A Bicentennial History. Hewlett: South Shore Record, 1976.

Writers Program of the Works Projects Administration [WPA] in the State of New York, compilers. *The Story of the Five Towns: Inwood, Lawrence, Cedarhurst, Woodmere, and Hewlett, Nassau County, Long Island.* Rockville Centre: Nassau Daily Review Star, 1941.

Centre Island

1. Cox, *Oyster Bay Town Records,* 1:624.

2. Berthold Fernow, ed., *Documents Relating to the Colonial History of the State of New York* (Albany: Weed, Parsons and Company, 1883), 14:435. Hereafter cited as Fernow, *Documents.*

3. Cox, *Oyster Bay Town Records,* 5:691, 8:65.

4. Benjamin F. Thompson, *History of Long Island; Containing An Account of the Discovery and Settlement; With Other Important and Interesting Matters to the Present Time* (New York: E. French, 1839), pp. 329-30. Hereafter cited as Thompson, *History of Long Island,* 1839.

5. On the history of Centre Island, see Malcolm MacKay and Charles G. Meyer, *A History of Centre Island* (Np: Privately printed, 1976).

Cold Spring Harbor

1. Tooker, *Indian Place-Names,* p. 277.

2. Cox, *Oyster Bay Town Records,* 1:4-5.

3. Walter K. Earle, *Out of the Wilderness* (Cold Spring Harbor: Whaling Museum Society, 1966), p. 14.

4. Romanah Sammis, *Huntington-Babylon Town History* (Huntington: Huntington Historical Society, 1937), p. 132.

5. Ibid., p. 119.

6. On the history of Cold Spring Harbor, see also:

   Valentine, Harriet G. *The Window to the Street,* 1981. Reprint; Cold Spring Harbor: Whaling Museum, 1991.

   Walton, Terry. *Cold Spring Harbor: Discovering History on Streets and Shores.* Cold Spring Harbor: Whaling Museum, 1999.

   Watson, Elizabeth L. *The Houses for Science: A Pictorial History of Cold Spring Harbor Laboratory.* Plainview: Cold Spring Harbor Laboratory Press, 1991.

Cove Neck

1. Cox, *Oyster Bay Town Records,* 1:3.

2. Hermann Hagedorn, *The Roosevelt Family of Sagamore Hill* (New York: Macmillan Company, 1954), p. 6.

3. Tooker, *Indian Place-Names,* pp. 220-21.

4. *Nassau Daily Review,* March 4, 1927.

East Hills

1. Roy W. Moger, *Roslyn: Then and Now* (Roslyn: Roslyn Public Schools, 1965), pp. 152, 154, 155, 156. (This book was revised by the author and reprinted by the Bryant Library in a 1992 edition edited by Myrna L. Sloam.)

2. Letter from East Hills Village Historian Catherine Hechler to the author, August 31, 1964.

3. Moger, *Roslyn, Then and Now,* p. 156.

4. Hechler to the author, August 31, 1964.

East Meadow

1. Hicks, *Hempstead Town Records,* 1:34.
2. Ibid., 1:41.
3. *Hempstead Inquirer,* November 16, 1836.
4. Hyde, *Atlas of Nassau County, Long Island, N.Y.,* 1914, p. 23; Hyde, *Real Estate Map of Nassau County, Long Island, N.Y.* (New York: E. Belcher Hyde, 1927), p. 4.
5. On the history of East Meadow, see East Meadow Public Library, *East Meadow: Its Past and Present, 1658-1976* (East Meadow: East Meadow Library, 1976); and Stephen Buczak, *East Meadow, 1914-1950,* 13 looseleaf vols. (North Bellmore: Stephen Buczak, 1989-1992), available in the Long Island Studies Institute at Hofstra University.

East Norwich

1. Cox, *Oyster Bay Town Records,* 1:63.
2. Richard Downing, *A Brief History of East Norwich, Long Island* (Syosset: Berry Hill Press, 1960), p. 3.
3. Cox, *Oyster Bay Town Records,* 2:57.
4. Downing, *Brief History of East Norwich,* p. 3.
5. Ibid., p. 3.
6. Secretary of State, *Manual for the Use of the Legislature of the State of New York for the Year 1849* (Albany: State Legislature, 1849), p. 70.
7. On the history of East Norwich, see also John E. Hammond, *Crossroads: A History of East Norwich* (Np: Privately printed, 1997).

East Rockaway

1. Fernow, *Documents,* 14:530.
2. J. Franklin Jameson, ed., *Narratives of New Netherlands 1609-1664* (New York: Charles Scribner's Sons, 1910), p. 230.
3. Tooker, *Indian Place-Names,* p. 214.
4. Hicks, *Hempstead Town Records,* 1:267.
5. *Picket,* May 1, 1868, December 17, 1869.
6. *South Side Observer,* March 18, 1892, March 25, 1892.
7. Ibid., September 1, 1893, December 22, 1893.
8. Ibid., July 26, 1895, August 30, 1895.
9. *Nassau Daily Review,* November 14, 1928.
10. Ibid., November 14, 1928.

East Williston

1. *Westbury Times,* March 14, 1925.
2. Hicks, *Hempstead Town Records,* 1:150; *Westbury Times,* March 14, 1925.
3. Seyfried, *Long Island Rail Road,* 3:203.
4. Ibid.
5. *Nassau Daily Review-Star,* October 24, 1951.
6. On the history of East Williston, see Nicholas A. Meyer and Cyril A. Lewis, *East Williston History, 1663-1978* (East Williston: Incorporated Village of East Williston, 1977).

Elmont

1. Hicks, *Hempstead Town Records,* 1:115.
2. *New York Daily News,* March 10, 1957.
3. *Long Island Democrat,* September 16, 1902.

4. *South Side Observer,* February 24, 1882.

5. Ibid.

6. *South Side Observer,* August 4, 1882.

7. On the history of Elmont, see *"Elmont's Our Home and We're Proud of It"* (Hempstead: Town of Hempstead, Department of Planning and Economic Development, [198?]).

Farmingdale

1. Gibbs, *Bethpage Bygones,* p. 8.

2. Cox, *Oyster Bay Town Records,* 7:398; 8:137, 138.

3. *Farmingdale Post,* March 9, 1955.

4. Manuscript by Jesse Merritt, in Nassau County Museum collections (Farmingdale vertical file), Long Island Studies Institute at Hofstra University.

5. Punk's Hole was an early name for present-day Manorville. Prime, *A History of Long Island,* p. 277.

6. *Nassau Daily Review,* May 25, 1936.

7. On the history of Farmingdale, see:

Johnston, William J., ed., "Farmingdale's History: A Reflection of Nassau County's First Century." *Nassau County: From Rural Hinterland to Suburban Metropolis,* edited by Joann P. Krieg and Natalie A. Naylor, forthcoming from the Long Island Studies Institute and Empire State Books.

——. ed. "The World War II Homefront: The Farmingdale Experience." *Long Island Forum* 58 (Summer 1995): 18-35.

Vining, Dorothy H., *Farmingdale, A Short History.* Farmingdale: Farmingdale Public Schools, 1983.

Floral Park

1. Seyfried, *Long Island Rail Road,* 2:91, 148.

2. Ibid., p. 117.

3. *Queens County Sentinel,* July 26, 1877.

4. Ibid., August 7, 1884; *Long Island Democrat,* August 12, 1884.

5. *Queens County Sentinel,* January 29, 1885, April 8, 1886.

6. *South Side Observer,* May 28, 1886.

7. Ibid., June 17, 1887.

8. *Queens County Sentinel,* June 2, 1887.

9. On the history of Floral Park, see Walter E. Gosden, ed., *Floral Park 75th Anniversary, 1908-1983* (Np., [1983?]).

Flower Hill

1. Hicks, *Hempstead Town Records,* 4:390-91.

2. Henry Onderdonk, Jr., *Documents and Letters Intended to Illustrate the Revolutionary Incidents of Queens County, N.Y.,* 2d series (New York: Leavitt and Company, 1846), p. 36. This book was reprinted in 1970 by the Ira J. Friedman Division of Kennikat Press.

3. Henry A. Stoutenburgh, *A Documentary History of the Dutch Congregation of Oyster Bay, Queens County, Island of Nassau* (New York: Knickerbocker Press, 1907), p. 255.

4. J. H. French, *Gazetteer of the State of New York* (Syracuse: R. P. Smith, 1860), p. 550. This *Gazetteer* has been reprinted a number of times, most recently by Genealogical Publishing in Baltimore in 1998.

5. *Port Washington News,* April 3, 1931, April 17, 1931.

6. Ibid., May 1, 1931.

Franklin Square

1. Bernice Schultz, *Colonial Hempstead, Long Island Life Under the Dutch and English* (Lynbrook: Nassau Daily Review-Star, 1937), p. 160. Hereafter cited as Schultz, *Colonial Hempstead.* (This book was reprinted in a 2d ed. under the name Bernice Schultz Marshall in 1962 by Ira J. Friedman in Port Washington.)

2. *Long Island Democrat,* February 15, 1842.

3. *Glen Cove Plaindealer,* July 11, 1851.

4. Schultz, *Colonial Hempstead,* p. 240.

5. *South Side Observer,* May 16, 1871.

6. *Nassau Daily Review,* February 27, 1929.

On the history of Franklin Square, see Paul Van Wie, *A History of Franklin Square and Environs: The Way It Was* (Franklin Square: Franklin Square Historical Society, 1994).

Freeport

1. Hicks, *Hempstead Town Records,* 1:112, 114.

2. Ibid., 3:222.

3. Prime, *History of Long Island,* p. 291.

4. *Hempstead Inquirer,* August 27, 1853.

5. Ibid.

6. Ibid

7. Letter from Freeport Village Historian Clinton E. Metz to the author, August 12, 1964.

On the history of Freeport, see Clinton E. Metz, *Freeport As It Was* (Np: Privately printed, 1976).

Garden City

1. Mildred H. Smith, *History of Garden City* (Manhasset: Channel Press, 1963), p. 18. This book was reprinted by the Garden City Historical Society in 1980.

2. Vincent F. Seyfried, *The Founding of Garden City, 1869-1893* (Garden City: Vincent F. Seyfried, 1969), p. 11.

3. Peter Ross and William S. Pelletreau, *A History of Long Island From Its Earliest Settlement to the Present Time* (New York: Lewis Historical Publishing Company, 1903), 2:96.

4. Smith, *History of Garden City,* p. 25.

5. Ibid., p. 28.

6. On the history of Garden City, see also M. H. Smith, *Garden City, Long Island in Early Photographs 1869-1919* (New York: Dover, 1987).

Garden City Park

1. Benjamin F. Thompson, *History of Long Island,* 1918. 3d ed., revised and enlarged by Charles J. Warren, 3 vols. (Reprint; Port Washington: I. J. Friedman, 1962), 2:31. Hereafter cited as Thompson, *History of Long Island,* 3d ed.

2. Horatio Gates Spafford, *A Gazetteer of the State of New York* (New York: H. C. Southwick, 1813), p. 255. This *Gazetteer* was reprinted by Heart of the Lakes Publishing in 1981.

3. Thomas F. Gordon, *Gazetteer of the State of New York* (Philadelphia: T. K. and P. G. Collins, 1836), p. 639.

4. *Hempstead Inquirer,* April 1, 1837.

5. Listing of maps on file in the Nassau County Clerk's office, Mineola, NY.

6. Seyfried, *Long Island Rail Road,* 3:188.

Glen Cove

1. Henry J. Scudder, *An Address Delivered at Glen Cove, L.I., at the Celebration of the Second Centennial Anniversary of the Settlement of that Village* (New York: New York Printing Company, 1868), pp. 18-19.

2. Tooker, *Indian Place-Names,* p. 145.

3. Cox, *Oyster Bay Town Records,* 1:42.

4. *East Norwich Enterprise,* June 26, 1897.

5. *Glen Cove Echo,* May 25, 1950.

6. *Hempstead Inquirer,* February 12, 1834.

7. Scudder, *Address Delivered at Glen Cove,* pp. 57, 58.

8. Ibid., pp. 57, 58.

9. Letter from Glen Cove City Clerk Kathleen Healy to the author, August 13, 1964.
On the history of Glen Cove, see:

  Coles, Robert R. *Glen Cove in the American Revolutionary War.* Glen Cove: Glen Cove Chamber of Commerce, 1976.

  Coles, Robert R., and Peter Luyster Van Santvoord. *A History of Glen Cove.* Glen Cove: Privately printed, 1967.

  DeRiggi, Mildred. "The Settlement of Muskitoe Cove, 1668-1700." M.A. thesis, University of Delaware, 1979.

Glen Head

1. Cox, *Oyster Bay Town Records,* 2:53.

2. *Hempstead Inquirer,* July 14, 1855.

3. Seyfried, *Long Island Rail Road,* 3:12.

4. *Glen Cove Gazette,* December 24, 1864, January 21, 1865.

5. Ibid., February 7, 1874.

6. Seyfried, *Long Island Rail Road,* 3:204.

Glenwood Landing

1. Cox, *Oyster Bay Town Records,* 1:135, 736.

2. Ibid., 1:328, 6:131, 352.

3. Ibid., 8:210.

4. Beers, *Atlas of Long Island,* 1873, p. 127.

5. *Sea Cliff News,* January 9, 1892, January 16, 1892, March 12, 1892.

Great Neck

1. Hicks, *Hempstead Town Records,* 1:142.

2. Tooker, *Indian Place-Names,* pp. 87, 116.

3. Hicks, *Hempstead Town Records,* 1:285.

4. Devah Spear and Gil Spear, *The Book of Great Neck* (Great Neck: Privately printed, 1936), p. 67. Hereafter cited as Spear, *Book of Great Neck.*

5. On the history of Great Neck, see also League of Women Voters of Great Neck, *This is Great Neck* (Great Neck: League of Women Voters of Great Neck, 1995).

Great Neck Estates

1. Hicks, *Hempstead Town Records,* 1:142.

2. Ibid., 1:285.

3. Spear, *Book of Great Neck,* p. 69.

4. Ibid.

Great Neck Plaza

1. Seyfried, *Long Island Rail Road,* 2:47, 147.

2. Richard Match, *Lucky Seven: A History of the Great Neck Public Schools* (Great Neck: Great Neck Public Schools, 1964), pp. 17-18.

3. Daniel Van Pelt, *Leslie's History of the Greater New York* (New York: Arkell Publishing Company, 1898), 3:373.

4. Letter from Great Neck Plaza Village Historian Martin A. Bursten to the author, September 9, 1964.

Greenvale

1. Cox, *Oyster Bay Town Records,* 2:53.

2. *Picket,* July 13, 1866; Seyfried, *Long Island Rail Road,* 3:12.

3. Ibid., p. 203.

4. *Queens County Sentinel,* June 10, 1897.

5. *East Norwich Enterprise,* September 4, 1897.

6. Ibid., November 12, 1902

7. Moger, *Roslyn, Then and Now,* p. 112.

8. Hyde, *Atlas of Nassau County,* 1914, p. 11.

Hempstead

1. Courtney R. Hall, "Early Days in Hempstead, Long Island," *New York History* 24 (October 1943): 537.

2. Thompson, *History of Long Island,* 1839, p. 342; Hicks, *Hempstead Town Records,* 1:7; Schultz, *Colonial Hempstead,* p. 12; and *Nassau Daily Star,* April 10, 1931. See also George D. A. Combes, "The Naming of Hempstead," *Nassau County Historical Society Journal* 29 (Summer/Fall 1969): 10-15.

3. Hall, *Early Days in Hempstead,* p. 4.

4. E. B. O'Callaghan, *History of New Netherland; or New York Under the Dutch,* 2 vols. (New York: D. Appleton, 1848), 1:317; John Romeyn Brodhead and E. B. O'Callaghan, eds., *Documents Relative to the Colonial History of the State of New York* (Albany: Weed, Parsons, 1856-1883), 14 vols.

5. *Nassau Daily Review,* October 31, 1929.

6. Hicks, *Hempstead Town Records,* 4:27.

7. Paul Bailey, ed., *Long Island, A History of Two Great Counties, Nassau and Suffolk,* 2 vols. (New York: Lewis Historical Publishing Company, 1949), 1:417.

8. *Hempstead Inquirer,* September 17, 1834.

9. On the history of the Village of Hempstead, see League of Women Voters, *Hempstead Village, Yesterday and Today* (Hempstead: League of Women Voters of the Town of Hempstead, 1975); and Sandra Schoenberg Kling, *A Demographic Profile of Hempstead Village, 1960-1985* (Hempstead: Hofstra University Center for Community Studies, 1985). See also histories of the Town of Hempstead which include information on the village, for example:

> *A History of the Town of Hempstead: The 325th Anniversary. . . 1644-1969.* Hempstead: Town of Hempstead, 1969.

> Marshall, Bernice Schultz. *Colonial Hempstead: Long Island Life Under the Dutch and English,* 1937. Reprint; Port Washington: I. J. Friedman, 1962.

> Naylor, Natalie A., ed. *The Roots and Heritage of Hempstead Town.* Interlaken, NY: Heart of the Lakes Publishing, 1994.

Herricks

1. Hicks, *Hempstead Town Records,* 6:460.
2. Ibid., 1:76.
3. New-York Historical Society, *Abstracts of Wills on File in the Surrogate's Office, City of New York, vol. 4, 1744-1753,* in *Collections of the New-York Historical Society for the Year 1895* (New York: New-York Historical Society), p. 389.

Hewlett

1. Hicks, *Hempstead Town Records,* 1:5; Seyfried, *Long Island Rail Road,* 1:80.
2. Seyfried, *Long Island Rail Road,* 1:25.
3. Ibid., p. 80.
4. *South Side Observer,* June 11, 1897.
5. Seyfried, *Long Island Rail Road,* 1:68.
6. Letter from John H. Galg to the author, August 16, 1967.
7. *South Side Observer,* February 17, 1893.
8. Ibid., February 19, 1897, June 11, 1897.
9. Ibid., June 12, 1896.
10. Alfred H. Bellot, *History of the Rockaways, From the Year 1685 to 1917* (Far Rockaway: Bellot's Histories, 1917), p. 64.
11. On the history of Hewlett, see also references to the Five Towns under Cedarhurst note no. 5.

Hewlett Bay Park

1. Bellot, *History of the Rockaways,* p. 64.
2. Letter from Hewlett Bay Park Village Clerk John F. Duncombe to the author, August 19, 1964.
3. *Woodmere-Hewlett Herald,* September 7, 1928.
On the history of Hewlett Bay Park, see Joel J. Morris, "Hewlett Bay Park: The Hunting Club Connection," *Nassau County Historical Society Journal* 49 (1994): 15-26.

Hewlett Harbor

1. Bellot, *History of the Rockaways,* p. 64.
2. Letter from Hewlett Harbor Village Clerk Louise Magaske to the author, August 19, 1964.
3. *Nassau Daily Review,* October 8, 1925.

Hewlett Neck

1. Letter from Hewlett Neck Village Clerk John F. Duncombe to the author, August 19, 1964.
2. Ibid.
3. *Nassau Daily Review,* January 5, 1927.
4. Letter from Duncombe, August 19, 1964.

Hicksville

1. Cox, *Oyster Bay Town Records,* 1:625.
2. Richard E. Evers, *Hicksville Today and Yesterday* (Hicksville: Hicksville Public Schools, 1962), p. 10.
3. Hicksville Tercentennial Committee, *Hicksville's Story, 300 Years of History 1648-1948* (Hicksville: Hicksville Tercentennial Committee, 1948), p. 11.
4. Evers, *Hicksville Today and Yesterday,* pp. 15, 17.

5. Ross and Pelletreau, *A History of Long Island*, 2:154; Munsell, *History of Queens County*, p. 549.

6. Evers, *Hicksville Today and Yesterday*, p. 17.

7. *South Side Observer*, October 13, 1893.

8. *East Norwich Enterprise*, October 21, 1893.

9. Ibid., October 5, 1895, September 26, 1896.

10. *East Norwich Enterprise*, February 26, 1921, April 30, 1921.

11. *Nassau Daily Review*, May 24, 1926, May 27, 1926.

12. On the history of Hicksville, see also:

    Brown, Dorothy R. *Good Old Hicksville*, 5 vols. Hicksville: Privately printed, [1989-1992?].

    Evers, Richard E. *The Story of Hicksville, Yesterday and Today*. Hicksville: Privately printed, 1978.

    Evers, Richard, and Anne Evers. "The Economic History of Hicksville," 4 vols. Typescript, spiral bound. Hicksville: Public Library, 1988-1996.

Inwood

1. Hicks, *Hempstead Town Records*, 1:132.

2. *South Side Observer*, October 6, 1871.

3. Ibid., January 4, 1889.

4. Ibid.

5. Ibid., March 1, 1889.

6. *Nassau Daily Star*, April 22, 1932.

7. *Nassau Daily Review-Star*, January 2, 1952.

8. On the history of Inwood, see references to the Five Towns under Cedarhurst, note no. 5.

Island Park

1. Hicks, *Hempstead Town Records*, 1:194.

2. *South Side Observer*, March 13, 1874.

3. Ibid., January 6, 1893.

4. Ibid.

5. Ibid., March 13, 1874.

6. Ibid., July 17, 1874.

7. Joann P. Krieg, "Barnum's Island, N.Y.: Fact or Fabrication," *New York Folklore* 10 (Winter-Spring 1984): 83-87.

8. Hazelton, *Boroughs of Brooklyn and Queens*, 1:406.

9. *South Side Observer*, July 13, 1900.

10. *East Norwich Enterprise*, July 20, 1901.

11. Letter from Island Park Village Clerk Harold J. Scully to the author, August 25, 1964.

12. *Nassau Daily Review*, November 6, 1926.

Island Trees

1. Hicks, *Hempstead Town Records*, 4:285.

2. Ibid., 3:156, 162.

3. Timothy Dwight, *Travels in New England and New York*, 4 vols. (London: William Baynes and Son, 1823), 3:306-7. This account was published posthumously; Dwight made the journey in 1804. Dwight's *Travels* was reprinted by Belknap Press of Harvard University Press in an edition edited by Barbara Miller Solomon in 1969. The quotation is on 3:225-26 in the 1969 edition.

Jericho

1. Cox, *Oyster Bay Town Records,* 1:625.

2. Henry Onderdonk, Jr., *The Annals of Hempstead 1643 to 1832* (Hempstead: Lott Van De Water, 1878), p. 98.

3. Cox, *Oyster Bay Town Records,* 1:708, 732, 734, 741.

4. Thompson, *History of Long Island,* 3d ed., 2:454.

5. Tooker, *Indian Place-Names,* p. 86.

6. *East Norwich Enterprise,* June 26, 1897.

7. Linda E. Braner, *The Mailman Cometh to Jericho* (East Hampton: East Hampton Star Press, 1960), p. 18.

8. Cox, *Oyster Bay Town Records,* 1:23.

9. Ibid., 1:608.

10. Braner, *Mailman Cometh to Jericho,* p. 1.

Kensington

1. Hicks, *Hempstead Town Records,* 1:142.

2. Tooker, *Indian Place-Names,* p. 87.

3. Hicks, *Hempstead Town Records,* 1:285.

4. Theodore C. Agins, *50th Anniversary, Incorporated Village of Kensington* (Kensington: Village of Kensington, 1959), p. 5.

5. Ibid., pp. 6-7.

Kings Point

1. Munsell, *History of Queens County,* p. 434.

2. Ibid., p. 434.

3. Ibid., p. 258.

4. Ross and Pelletreau, *History of Long Island,* 2:593.

5. Hicks, *Hempstead Town Records,* 3:383.

6. Letter from King's Point Village Clerk Mirian D. Dale to the author, August 27, 1964.

7. *Port Washington News,* November 14, 1924.

Lake Success

1. Tooker, *Indian Place-Names,* p. 220.

2. Thompson, *History of Long Island,* 3d ed., 2:60.

3. Hicks, *Hempstead Town Records,* 1:314.

4. French, *Gazetteer,* p. 550.

5. Prime, *History of Long Island,* p. 295.

6. Letter from Lake Success Village Historian Mrs. P. Schuyler Van Bloem to the author, August 18, 1964.

On the history of Lake Success, see Kate Van Bloem, *History of the Village of Lake Success* (Lake Success: Incorporated Village of Lake Success [1968]).

Lakeview

1. Henry Onderdonk, Jr., *Queens County in Olden Times* (Jamaica: Charles Welling, 1865), p. 50.

2. *Census of the State of New York for 1865* (Albany: Charles Van Benthuysen, 1867), p. 54.

3. Albert B. Corey, "Meaning of Schodack," *Long Island Forum* 20 (February 1957): 20.

4. *Hempstead Inquirer,* February 21, 1863.

5. Seyfried, *Long Island Rail Road*, 1:49.
6. *South Side Observer*, November 13, 1903.
7. Ibid., July 21, 1905.
8. *Newsday*, September 14, 1988.

Lattingtown

1. Cox, *Oyster Bay Town Records*, 1:732.
2. Ibid., p. 5.
3. Letter from Lattingtown Village Historian Helen Dudgeon to the author, September 1, 1964.
4. Cox, *Oyster Bay Town Records*, 5:326, 6:562.
5. Letter from Dudgeon, September 1, 1964.
6. Ibid.

Laurel Hollow

1. Tooker, *Indian Place-Names*, p. 277.
2. Cox, *Oyster Bay Town Records*, 1:124.
3. Beers, *Atlas of Long Island*, 1873, p. 128.
4. Estelle Valentine Newman, "Cold Spring Harbor Hotels," *Long Island Forum* 13 (November 1950): 207.
5. Beers, *Atlas of Long Island*, 1873, p. 128.
6. *Nassau Daily Review*, June 14, 1935.
7. Ibid.
8. Ibid., December 21, 1935.

Lawrence

1. Seyfried, *Long Island Rail Road*, 1:80.
2. Bellot, *History of the Rockaways*, p. 73.
3. Ibid.
4. Seyfried, *Long Island Rail Road*, 1:80.
5. *Hempstead Inquirer*, July 23, 1886.
6. Bellot, *History of the Rockaways*, p. 75.
7. On the history of Lawrence, see [Milton Meyer], *Village of Lawrence, N.Y.: A Brief History of a Long Island Community* (Village of Lawrence, 1977); and references to the Five Towns under Cedarhurst, note no. 5.

Lawrence Beach

1. Bellot, *History of the Rockaways*, p. 74.
2. Ibid., p. 74.
3. Ibid., p. 74.

Levittown

1. Hicks, *Hempstead Town Records*, 4:285.
2. Dwight, *Travels in New-England and New York*, 3:306-7.
3. *Nassau Daily Review-Star*, December 12, 1951.
4. Ibid.
5. *Levittown Tribune*, January 29, 1948.
6. Levittown has been the subject of many studies. See, for example:
   Buhr, Jenni. "Levittown as a Utopian Community." In *Long Island: The Suburban Experience*, edited by Barbara M. Kelly, pp. 67-78. Interlaken, NY: Heart of the Lakes, 1990.

Keller, Mollie. "Levittown and the Transformation of the Metropolis." Ph.D. diss., New York University, 1990. Copy in the Long Island Studies Institute, Hofstra University.

Kelly, Barbara M. *Expanding the American Dream: Building and Rebuilding Levittown.* Albany: State University of New York, 1993.

——. "Levittown: Opening a New Frontier." *Nassau County Historical Society Journal* 47 (1992): 13-21.

Liell, John. "Levittown: A Study in Community Planning and Development." Ph.D. diss., Yale University, 1952. Copy in the Long Island Studies Institute, Hofstra University.

Matarrese, Lynne. *History of Levittown, New York.* Levittown: Levittown Historical Society, 1998.

Newsday. "Levittown at Fifty." *Newsday,* Supplement, September 18, 1997, sec. H. Portions are included in Newsday, *Long Island: Our Story,* pp. 404-19. Melville: Newsday, 1998.

Locust Valley

1. Cox, *Oyster Bay Town Records,* 1:141.
2. Tooker, *Indian Place-Names,* p. 40.
3. *East Norwich Enterprise,* December 19, 1914.
4. Ibid.
5. Cox, *Oyster Bay Town Records,* 5:304.
6. *Glen Cove Gazette,* December 26, 1857.
7. Chapman Publishing, *Portrait and Biographical Record of Queens County, Long Island, New York* (New York: Chapman Publishing, 1896), p. 959. Hereafter cited as Chapman, *Portrait and Biographical Record.*
8. *Glen Cove Gazette,* December 26, 1857.
9. *East Norwich Enterprise,* December 19, 1914.
10. Ibid., February 1, 1902.

Long Beach

1. Hazelton, *Boroughs of Brooklyn and Queens,* 2:880.
2. Hicks, *Hempstead Town Records,* 6:270.
3. Hazelton, *Boroughs of Brooklyn and Queens,* 2:880.
4. *South Side Observer,* January 27, 1893.
5. Hazelton, *Boroughs of Brooklyn and Queens,* 2:885-86.
6. Letter from Long Beach City Manager Foster E. Vogel to the author, August 27, 1964.

On the history of Long Beach, see *1922-1997, Long Beach: The Early Years* (Long Beach: City of Long Beach, 1997); and Roberta M. Fiore and Liz Coffin Allerhand, "Sand Bar to City: William H. Reynolds and the Planned Community of Long Beach 1906-1922," in *Nassau County: From Rural Hinterland to Suburban Metropolis,"* edited by Joann P. Krieg and Natalie A. Naylor, forthcoming from the Long Island Studies Institute and Empire State Books.

Lynbrook

1. *Long Island Democrat,* February 1, 1853.
2. Steven J. Willner, *Lynbrook Legacy, The Story of Our Community* (Valley Stream: Maileader Publishing Corp., n.d.), p. 4.
3. Seyfried, *Long Island Rail Road,* 1:77.
4. *South Side Observer,* February 12, 1891, February 26, 1891.
5. Ibid., March 4, 1892, March 11, 1892.

6. Ibid., August 11, 1893, August 18, 1893, April 13, 1894, May 4, 1894.

7. *Nassau Daily Review-Star,* November 16, 1939.

8. Ibid., August 16, 1928.

Malverne

1. Seyfried, *Long Island Rail Road,* 1:48.

2. *Nassau Daily Star,* August 17, 1933.

3. Ibid.

4. George R. Van Allen, *The Rise of Malverne* (Amityville: Long Island Forum, 1955), p. 2.

5. *South Side Observer,* March 14, 1913.

6. *Nassau Daily Review-Star,* April 2, 1947; and *Malverne Herald,* May 20, 1948.

7. *Nassau Daily Review-Star,* April 2, 1947.

On the history of Malverne, see also Gerard J. Janeske, *Malverne: The Story of Its Years* (Malverne: Incorporated Village of Malverne, 1972).

Manhasset

1. Hicks, *Hempstead Town Records,* 1:263.

2. *Hempstead Inquirer,* February 1, 1837.

3. Ibid., February 22, 1837; and *Long Island Democrat,* March 1, 1837.

4. *Long Island Democrat,* March 8, 1837.

5. *Hempstead Inquirer,* July 1, 1837.

6. *Long Island Democrat,* July 5, 1837.

7. Tooker, *Indian Place-Names,* p. 93.

8. *Long Island Democrat,* October 31, 1843.

On the history of Manhasset, see Manhasset Chamber of Commerce, *Manhasset: The First 300 Years* (Manhasset: Chamber of Commerce, 1980).

Manorhaven

1. Hicks, *Hempstead Town Records,* 7:266.

2. Beers, *Atlas of Long Island,* 1873, p. 8.

3. *East Norwich Enterprise,* February 17, 1894.

4. Hyde, *Atlas of Nassau County, N.Y.,* 1914, p. 8.

5. *North Hempstead Record,* May 12, 1926.

6. Ibid.

7. *Port Washington News,* September 12, 1930.

Massapequa

1. Tooker, *Indian Place-Names,* pp. 111-12.

2. Cox, *Oyster Bay Town Records,* 1:347-48, 3:161.

3. French, *Gazetteer,* p. 550.

4. *South Side Observer,* July 22, 1887, July 27, 1888.

5. *Queens County Sentinel,* July 14, 1887.

6. *South Side Observer,* January 18, 1889.

7. On the history of Massapequa, see Barbara F. Cahn, *An Illustrated History of Massapequa,* 2d ed. (Massapequa: Massapequa Publishing Co., 1968); and the Historical Society of the Massapequas, *Historical Society of Massapequa Celebrates the Anniversaries* (Massapequa: Historical Society of the Massapequas, 1981).

Massapequa Park

1. Seyfried, *Long Island Rail Road,* 1:78.

2. Barbara F. Cahn, ed., *An Illustrated History of Massapequa* (Massapequa: Massapequa Publishing Co., 1961), p. 46. (A revised 2d edition was issued in 1968.)

3. Hyde, *Real Estate Map of Nassau County, N.Y.,* 1923, p. 6.

4. Cahn, *Illustrated History of Massapequa,* p. 46.

5. Letter from Michael J. Brady to the author, October 12, 1964.

Matinecock

1. Fernow, *Documents,* 14:56. See also "Indian Deeds," in *Roots and Heritage of Hempstead Town,* ed. Naylor, pp. 174, 177 n. 2.

2. Tooker, *Indian Place-Names,* p. 116.

3. *East Norwich Enterprise,* June 26, 1897.

4. *Nassau Daily Review,* March 29, 1928.

5. On the history of Matinecock, see George William Cocks, "Old Matinecock," *Nassau County Historical Society Journal* 22 (Fall 1961): 1-11.

Merrick

1. Fernow, *Documents,* 14:530.

2. Charles N. Kent, *An Historical Sketch of Merrick, Long Island, 1643-1900* (Merrick: Merrick Library, 1900), p. 14.

3. Tooker, *Indian Place-Names,* pp. 126-27.

4. *Long Island Democrat,* October 31, 1843.

5. On the history of Merrick, see also the Historical Society of the Merricks, *Memories of the Merricks* (Merrick: Merrick Historical Society, 1977).

Mill Neck

1. Cox, *Oyster Bay Town Records,* 1:40-41.

2. Ibid., 2:47-49.

3. Ibid., 4:686-87.

4. *Nassau Daily Review,* March 5, 1925.

On the history of Mill Neck, see Dorothy Horton McGee, "Historical Sketches of Mill Neck," *Long Island Courant* 2 (March 1960): 7-38.

Mineola

1. Mildred H. Smith, *Early History of the Long Island Railroad,* p. 6.

2. *Hempstead Inquirer,* October 3, 1840.

3. Ibid., January 24, 1846.

4. Letter from Postmaster K. P. Aldrich to Nassau County Historian Jesse Merritt, April 1944 in Nassau County Museum collection (Mineola vertical file), Long Island Studies Institute at Hofstra University.

5. *Hempstead Inquirer,* March 12, 1859.

6. *Nassau Daily Review,* March 7, 1924.

7. *Hempstead Inquirer,* March 12, 1859.

8. Quoted in *Nassau Daily Review,* March 7, 1924. George Stewart attributes "Minneola" (with Mineola as a varient spelling) to the Siouan (Sioux), meaning "much water" (*American Place Names,* p. 297).

Munsey Park

1. *Hempstead Inquirer,* July 1, 1837.

2. *Nassau Daily Review,* November 23, 1922.

3. *New York Sun,* April 9, 1932.

4. *Brooklyn Daily Times,* January 31, 1932.

5. *New York Sun,* April 9, 1932.

6. Munsey Park Association, *Munsey Park at Manhasset* (New York: Munsey Park Association, n.d.), p. 2.

7. *Brooklyn Daily Times,* January 31, 1932.

Munson

1. *South Side Observer,* May 16, 1871.

2. *Queens County Sentinel,* May 16, 1895.

3. *Long Island Democrat,* May 28, 1895.

4. Ross and Pelletreau, *History of Long Island,* 3:100.

5. *Long Island Democrat,* September 15, 1895.

6. *Queens County Sentinel,* August 15, 1895.

Muttontown

1. Cox, *Oyster Bay Town Records,* 6:641, 736.

2. Ibid, 8:141.

3. Hyde, *Real Estate Map of Nassau County,* 1927, p. 2.

4. *Oyster Bay Guardian,* July 31, 1931.

5. Ibid.

6. *Oyster Bay Guardian,* September 26, 1931.

New Cassel

1. Seyfried, *Long Island Rail Road,* 3:188.

2. Philip B. Gove, ed., *Webster's Seventh New Collegiate Dictionary* (Springfield, MA: Merriam Company, 1965) p. 1127.

3. *East Norwich Enterprise,* May 16, 1885.

4. *Roslyn News,* October 30, 1886.

5. *Westbury Record,* August 16, 1956.

6. *South Side Observer,* April 17, 1891.

7. *East Norwich Enterprise,* April 11, 1891.

8. *New Cassel Notes,* April 4, 1950.

New Hyde Park

1. Hicks, *Hempstead Town Records,* 1:485.

2. *Brooklyn Daily Eagle,* August 25, 1918.

3. Ibid.

4. Ibid.

5. Onderdonk, *Queens County in Olden Times,* p. 100.

6. William Cobbett, *A Year's Residence in America* (Boston: Small, Maynard and Company, n.d. [1819?]), p. 43. This book has been reprinted in different editions including by the University of Illinois in 1965.

7. Letter from Jesse Merritt to Lester G. Peck, February 12, 1957, in Nassau County Museum collection (New Hyde Park vertical file), Long Island Studies Institute at Hofstra University.

8. Seyfried, *Long Island Rail Road,* 3:187-88.

9. Henry J. Lee, ed., *The Long Island Almanac and Year Book, 1928* (Brooklyn: Brooklyn Daily Eagle, 1928), p. 70.

On the history of New Hyde Park, see Charlotte Henry, compiler, "Hyde Park, Home of Long Island's Colonial Gentry (The Early Days of New Hyde Park)," typescript photocopy, 1994 (copy in the Long Island Studies Institute, Hofstra University); and George E. Christ, *The Early History of New Hyde Park* (New Hyde Park: Privately printed, 1997).

North Bellmore

1. Munsell, *History of Queens County,* p. 169.
2. *Hempstead Inquirer,* March 23, 1850.
3. Ibid., December 25, 1858.
4. *Picket,* April 19, 1867.
5. *South Side Observer,* July 18, 1919, October 5, 1919.

North Hills

1. Beers, *Atlas of Long Island,* 1873, p. 123.
2. Letter from J. Oakey McKnight to the author, August 18, 1964.
3. Ibid.
4. Ibid.

North Merrick

1. Letter from Norbert Johnson to the author, June 29, 1967.
2. Ibid.
3. *Merrick Life,* July 1, 1976.

North New Hyde Park

1. *Hempstead Inquirer,* November 6, 1858.
2. Hyde, *Map of Long Island,* 1896, p. 4.
3. Letter from postmaster Andrew A. Wulforst to the author, August 10, 1967.

Oceanside

1. Rev. William H. Moore, *History of St. George's Church, Hempstead, Long Island, N.Y.* (New York: E. P. Dutton & Company, 1881), p. 54.
2. Hicks, *Hempstead Town Records,* 1:103.
3. Moore, *History of St. George's Church,* pp. 53, 173, 204, 215.
4. *South Side Observer,* September 3, 1880.
5. Ibid., November 23, 1880, April 8, 1881.
6. Ibid., December 19, 1890, December 2, 1892.
7. On the history of Oceanside, see Aleph Zadik Alepha, *The First History of Oceanside* (Oceanside: First United Methodist Church, 1975).

Old Bethpage

1. Gibbs, *Bethpage Bygones,* p. 8.
2. Cox, *Oyster Bay Town Records,* 2:212.
3. *Babylon Town Leader,* March 23, 1961.
4. *Nassau Daily Review,* April 14, 1936.
5. On the history of Old Bethpage, see Richard Koubek, compiler, *Our Town: Plainview-Old Bethpage Community Studies Resource Portfolio* (Plainview: Plainview-Old Bethpage Central School District, 1987). A copy is in the Long Island Studies Institute collections, Hofstra University.

Old Brookville

1. Cox, *Oyster Bay Town Records,* 1:79.
2. Tooker, *Indian Place-Names,* p. 251.
3. Cox, *Oyster Bay Town Records,* 3:503.
4. Shelley, *John Underhill,* p. 1.
5. Cox, *Oyster Bay Town Records,* 4:674.
6. *Long Island Farmer,* February 8, 1848.
7. Ibid., February 29, 1848, March 7, 1848.

8. *Oyster Bay Guardian,* November 15, 1929.

9. Ibid., December 27, 1929.

Old Westbury

1. Jacqueline Overton, *Long Island's Story* (Garden City: Doubleday, Doran and Company, 1929), p. 166. (This book was reprinted in 1961 in a 2d edition by Ira J. Friedman in Port Washington with a sequel, "The Rest of The Story, 1929-1961," by Bernice Marshall.)

2. Tooker, *Indian Place-Names,* pp. 269-70.

3. Hicks, *Hempstead Town Records,* 1:150, 300.

4. Overton, *Long Island's Story,* p. 166.

5. *Westbury Times,* March 14, 1925.

6. Hicks, *Hempstead Town Records,* 1:468.

7. *Hempstead Inquirer,* January 23, 1841.

8. *East Norwich Enterprise,* November 23, 1907.

9. Munsell, *History of Queens County,* p. 65.

10. *Picket,* April 10, 1868.

11. *Long Island Democrat,* March 28, 1882.

12. On the history of Old Westbury, see Marietta Hicks, "Old Westbury and Jericho—A Closely Knit Quaker Community," typescript. c. 1940 [?]. A copy is in the Nassau County Museum collection, Long Island Studies Institute, Hofstra University.

Oyster Bay

1. Jameson, *Narratives of New Netherlands,* p. 202.

2. French, *Gazetteer,* p. 550; *Hempstead Inquirer,* January 24, 1846.

3. *Hempstead Inquirer,* January 24, 1846.

4. Tooker, *Indian Place-Names,* pp. 255-56.

5. French, *Gazetteer,* p. 550.

6. On the history of Oyster Bay, see Van S. Merle-Smith, Jr., *The Village of Oyster Bay, Its Founding and Growth From 1653 to 1700* (Garden City: Privately printed, 1953); and Frances Irvin, "Oyster Bay in History," typescript, 1960. Copy in the Nassau County Museum collection, Long Island Studies Institute at Hofstra University.

Oyster Bay Cove

1. Cox, *Oyster Bay Town Records,* 1:241.

2. *Nassau Daily Review,* November 12, 1931.

3. Letter from Oyster Bay Cove Village Trustee Grover O'Neill to the author, August 20, 1964.

On pre-Revoluntionary rural life in Oyster Bay Cove, see *The Diary of Mary Cooper: Life on a Long Island Farm, 1768-1773,* edited by Field Horne (Oyster Bay: Oyster Bay Historical Society, 1981).

Plainedge

1. Hicks, *Hempstead Town Records,* 1:300.

2. Ibid., p. 150.

3. Gibbs, *Bethpage Bygones,* p. 8.

4. Martha B. Flint, *Early Long Island, A Colonial Study* (New York: G. P. Putnam's Sons, 1896), p. 74. This book was reprinted under the title *Long Island Before the Revolution: A Colonial Study* (Port Washington: Ira J. Friedman, 1967).

5. Cox, *Oyster Bay Town Records,* 7:398.

6. Prime, *History of Long Island,* p. 278.

7. Iris Gibbs, "Building a School in 1878," *Long Island Forum* 11 (October 1948): 187.

Plainview

1. Tooker, *Indian Place-Names,* p. 99.
2. Gabriel Furman, *Antiquities of Long Island* (New York: J. W. Bouton, 1874), pp. 62-63. (This work was published posthumously; Furman had died in 1856. The book was reprinted by Ira J. Friedman in Port Washington in 1968.)
3. Tooker, *Indian Place-Names,* p. 99.
4. *East Norwich Enterprise,* March 13, 1886.
5. Ibid.
On the history of Plainview, see Koubeck, *Our Town: Plainview-Old Bethpage.*

Plandome

1. Thompson, *History of Long Island,* 3d ed., 3:563.
2. Ibid.
3. William S. Thomas, "Incidents in Plandome History," *Nassau County Historical Society Journal* 11 (Autumn 1948): 22.
4. Onderdonk, *Queens County in Olden Times,* p. 94.
5. Thomas, "Incidents in Plandome History," p. 22.

Plandome Heights

1. Hicks, *Hempstead Town Records,* 1:263.
2. *Hempstead Inquirer,* February 1, 1837; *Long Island Democrat,* March 1, 1837; *Hempstead Inquirer,* July 1, 1837.
3. Onderdonk, *Queens County in Olden Times,* p. 94.
4. Letter from Plandome Heights Village Clerk Grace S. Tannehill to the author, November 7, 1964.
5. *Port Washington News,* February 8, 1929.
6. Ibid.
7. Letter from Tannehill, November 7, 1964.

Plandome Manor

1. Hyde, *Atlas of Nassau County,* 1914, pp. 8, 52.
2. Hyde, *Real Estate Map of Nassau County,* 1923, p. 1.
3. *Manhasset Mail,* August 18, 1932.
4. On the history of Plandome Manor, see Beatrice A. Tusiani, "A Complete History of Plandome Manor," parts 1 and 2, *Long Island Forum* 44 (July/August 1981): 132-41, 168-73.

Point Lookout

1. Daniel M. Tredwell, *Personal Reminiscences of Men and Things on Long Island,* 2 vols. (Brooklyn: Charles Andrew Ditmas, 1912), 2:206-7.
2. Ibid.
3. Letter from Mrs. Norman Mellon to the author, September 26, 1967.
4. *Nassau County Review,* August 5, 1904; *South Side Observer,* May 10, 1918.
5. *North Hempstead Record,* May 17, 1918.
6. Letter from Mrs. Mellon, September 26, 1967.

Port Washington

1. Hicks, *Hempstead Town Records,* 1:263.
2. Fernow, *Documents,* 14:15.

3. Tooker, *Indian Place-Names,* p. 244.

4. Hicks, *Hempstead Town Records,* 5:85.

5. *Hempstead Inquirer,* July 2, 1859.

6. Schultz, *Colonial Hempstead,* p. 169.

7. *North Shore Daily Journal,* April 19, 1935.

8. Charlotte E. Merriman, *Tales of Sint Sink* (Port Washington: Board of Education of Port Washington, NY, 1935), p. 225. (This book was reprinted by the Cow Neck Peninsula Historical Society in 1965.)

9. *Hempstead Inquirer,* July 2, 1859.

10. *Port Washington News,* April 1, 1932.

On the history of Port Washington, see also:

> *Cow Neck Peninsula Historical Society Journal,* 1965 to date.

> Shodell, Elly. *Flight of Memory: Long Island's Aeronautical Past.* Port Washington: Port Washington Library, 1995.

> ———. *Particles of the Past: Sandmining on Long Island in the 1870's-1980's.* Port Washington: Port Washington Public Library, 1985.

> Williams, George L. "The L.I.R.R. and Community Transportation—The Development of Port Washington 1900-1915." Parts 1 and 2. *Long Island Forum* 60 (Spring 1997): 4-16; 60 (Summer 1997): 30-42.

> ———. Lower Main Street: A Waterfront Community. Port Washington: Landmarks Committee, Cow Neck Peninsula Historical Society, 1982.

> ———. *Port Washington in the Twentieth Century: Places and People.* Port Washington: Landmarks Committee, Cow Neck Peninsula Historical Society, 1982.

Port Washington North

1. *Port Washington News,* April 1, 1932.

2. Ibid.

3. Ibid., May 20, 1932.

4. Ibid.

5. Ibid., July 8, 1932, August 5, 1932.

Rockville Centre

1. Prime, *History of Long Island,* p. 287 .

2. *Nassau Daily Star,* April 11, 1930.

3. Ibid.

4. *Hempstead Inquirer,* August 27, 1847.

5. *South Side Observer,* June 2, 1882.

6. Floyd B. Watson, *History of Rockville Centre Public Schools and Some Early History of Rockville Centre* (Rockville Centre: Acorn Publishing Company, 1952), pp. 10-11.

7. *Hempstead Inquirer,* February 10, 1849, February 17, 1849.

8. *South Side Observer,* May 5, 1882, June 9, 1882.

9. Hazelton, *Boroughs of Brooklyn and Queens,* 2:877.

10. *Nassau Daily Review,* November 3, 1924.

11. On the history of Rockville Centre, see also Preston R. Bassett and Arthur L. Hodges, *The History of Rockville Centre* (Uniondale: Salisbury Printers, 1969).

Roosevelt

1. Writers' Program of the Works Projects Administration [WPA] in the State of New York, "The Story of Roosevelt, Nassau County, Long Island," typescript, p. 2.

Copy in Nassau County Museum collection (pamphlet file), Long Island Studies Institute at Hofstra University.

2. Prime, *History of Long Island,* p. 292.

3. French, *Gazetteer,* p. 547.

4. *Nassau County Review,* February 14, 1902.

5. Ibid.

6. Ibid., March 7, 1902.

7. Ibid.

Roslyn

1. Hicks, *Hempstead Town Records,* 1:47.

2. *Long Island Farmer,* September 17, 1844.

3. Thompson, *History of Long Island,* 3d ed., 2:560-61.

4. Moger, *Roslyn, Then and Now,* p. vi.

5. Ibid.

6. *Long Island Farmer,* November 19, 1844.

7. Letter from Roslyn Village Clerk Barbara R. Moreland to the author, August 17, 1964.

Roslyn Estates

1. Letter from Louis O. Rohland to the author, August 19, 1964.

2. The Association is believed to be the oldest such organization of its type. Telephone conversation with Ruth J. Hinrichs, Historian of Roslyn Estates, May 27, 1999.

3. Letter from Rohland, August 19, 1964.

Roslyn Harbor

1. *Long Island Farmer,* September 17, 1844.

2. Hyde, *Real Estate Map of Nassau County,* 1923, p. 3.

3. Letter from Louis O. Rohland to the author, August 19, 1964.

4. Conrad Godwin Goddard, *The Early History of Roslyn Harbor, Long Island* (Roslyn Harbor: Conrad Godwin Goddard, 1972), p. 3.

Roslyn Heights

1. *East Norwich Enterprise,* October 22, 1892.

2. Letter from Louis O. Rohland to the author, August 19, 1964.

3. Ibid.

4. *Roslyn News,* July 27, 1967.

5. Moger, *Roslyn, Then and Now,* p. 138.

Russell Gardens

1. Letter from Francis H. Knighton to the author, June 26, 1966.

2. Ibid.

3. Spear, *The Book of Great Neck,* p. 77.

4. Letter from Knighton, June 26, 1966.

5. Ibid.

6. Spear, *The Book of Great Neck,* p. 77.

Saddle Rock

1. Hicks, *Hempstead Town Records,* 1:142, 285.

2. Ibid., 2:149.

3. Spear, *The Book of Great Neck,* p. 68.

4. Letter from Saddle Rock Village Clerk Louis Kurke to the author, August 21, 1964.

Sands Point

1. Hicks, *Hempstead Town Records,* 1:263.
2. Ibid., 1:214, 3:349-51.
3. Thompson, *History of Long Island,* 3d ed., 3:583-84.
4. Hicks, *Hempstead Town Records,* 7:29.
5. Ibid., 7:9.
6. *Port Washington News,* September 24, 1910.
7. On the history of Sands Point, see Sands Point Civic Association, *Sands Point* (Sands Point: Sands Point Civic Association, 1979).

Sea Cliff

1. Coles and Van Santvoord, *History of Glen Cove,* p. 8.
2. Cox, *Oyster Bay Town Records,* 1:636.
3. Ibid., 1:269.
4. Ibid., 8:392.
5. Munsell, *History of Queens County,* p. 526.
6. Ibid., p. 529.
7. Ibid.
8. *South Side Observer,* September 21, 1883.
9. On the history of Sea Cliff, see Frank O. Braynard and Anthony Brescia, eds., *The Village of Sea Cliff, 100 Years* (Sea Cliff: Sea Cliff Centennial Commission, 1983).

Seaford

1. *Hempstead Inquirer,* April 7, 1838.
2. Seyfried, *Long Island Rail Road,* 1:78.
3. *Long Island Democrat,* January 9, 1849.
4. *Hempstead Inquirer,* January 3, 1868.
5. John H. Jones, *The Jones Family of Long Island, Descendants of Major Thomas Jones 1665-1726 and Allied Families* (New York: Tobias A. Wright, 1907), p. 162.
6. *Southeast Nassau Enterprise,* February 28, 1963.

Searingtown

1. Hicks, *Hempstead Town Records,* 1:7, 4:170.
2. Ibid., 4:170, 5:236.
3. Searingtown Methodist Episcopal Church, *150th Anniversary of the Searingtown Methodist Episcopal Church, 1785-1935* (Searingtown, 1935), p. 2. The Searing Memorial United Methodist Church merged with the Roslyn United Methodist Church in 1979, resulting in the addition of Roslyn to the church name. Mergers of denominations on the national level in 1939 and 1968 had created the United Methodist Church. (Information from Bert Bradley, Searing-Roslyn United Methodist Church, August 17, 1999.)

South Floral Park

1. Manuscript of records in the Nassau County Clerk's Office, Mineola.
2. Letter from South Floral Park Village Clerk Jeanne Russac to the author, September 30, 1964.
3. *Nassau Daily Review,* November 6, 1925.
4. Letter from Russac, September 30, 1964.

Stewart Manor

1. Smith, *History of Garden City,* pp. 18, 28.
2. *Hempstead Inquirer,* February 5, 1915.
3. Ibid.
4. Stewart Manor Anniversary Committee, *Silver Anniversary of the Village of Stewart Manor 1927-1952* (Stewart Manor: Stewart Manor Anniversary Committee, 1952), p. 5.
5. Letter from Stewart Manor Village Clerk C. M. Jackson to the author, August 14, 1964.

On the history of Stewart Manor, see also *Golden Anniversary of the Village of Stewart Manor, 1927-1977* (Stewart Manor: Village of Stewart Manor, 1977).

Syosset

1. Cox, *Oyster Bay Town Records,* 8:69.
2. Ibid., pp. 91, 139.
3. French, *Gazetteer,* p. 550; *Hempstead Inquirer,* January 24, 1846.
4. Tooker, *Indian Place-Names,* pp. 255-56.
5. *Hempstead Inquirer,* January 24, 1846.

On the history of Syosset, see Patricia A. Tunison, *Looking Back on Syosset* (Syosset, 1975).

Thomaston

1. Hicks, *Hempstead Town Records,* 1:142, 285.
2. Seyfried, *Long Island Rail Road,* 2:47, 147.
3. Match, *History of the Great Neck Public Schools,* pp. 17-18.
4. Daniel Van Pelt, *Leslie's History of the Greater New York,* 3:373.
5. Spear, *The Book of Great Neck,* p. 71.
6. Letter from Thomaston Village Clerk Benton R. Gallagher to the author, August 13, 1964.

On the history of Thomaston, see Thomaston Village, *Incorporated Village of the Village of Thomaston* (Great Neck, 1976).

Uniondale

1. Hicks, *Hempstead Town Records,* 1:40.
2. Ibid., 6:21.
3. *Plaindealer,* May 13, 1853.
4. *Hempstead Inquirer,* May 14, 1853.
5. *East Norwich Enterprise,* November 16, 1895.
6. *Queens County Sentinel,* December 20, 1888.
7. *Nassau County Review,* August 9, 1901.

University Gardens

1. Tooker, *Indian Place-Names,* p. 220.
2. Thompson, *History of Long Island,* 3d ed., 2:60; Tooker, *Indian Place-Names,* p. 220; Hicks, *Hempstead Town Records,* 1:314.
3. French, *Gazetteer,* p. 550.
4. *North Hempstead Record,* May 19, 1926.
5. Ibid.
6. Hyde, *Real Estate Map of Nassau County,* 1927, p. 3.

Upper Brookville
1. Cox, *Oyster Bay Town Records,* 1:79.
2. Tooker, *Indian Place-Names,* pp. 250-51.
3. Cox, *Oyster Bay Town Records,* 1:7, 3:503.
4. Shelley, *John Underhill,* p. 1.
5. Cox, *Oyster Bay Town Records,* 4:674.
6. *Long Island Farmer,* February 8, 1848.
7. Ibid., February 29, 1948, March 7, 1948.
8. Letter from Upper Brookville Village Historian Mrs. James G. Dartt to the author, October 29, 1964.

On the history of Upper Brookville, see John Lang Rawlinson, *The History of Upper Brookville, 1932-1982* (Upper Brookville: Board of Trustees, [1982?]).

Valley Stream
1. *Nassau Daily Star,* August 16, 1928.
2. *Picket,* January 28, 1870.
3. Ibid., April 1, 1870.
4. Letter from Valley Stream Village Clerk Carl F. Kappauf to the author, August 13, 1964.
5. *Nassau Daily Star,* August 3, 1933.
6. *South Side Observer,* July 28, 1905.
7. *Nassau Daily Star,* August 3, 1933.
8. On the history of Valley Stream, see Alonzo Gibbs, "Profile of a Long Island Town," (Valley Stream in the early 1920s), *Nassau County Historical Society Journal* 29 (Winter-Spring, 1969): 10-17; and Howard F. Ruehl, *History of Valley Stream, 1840-1975* (Valley Stream: Incorporated Village of Valley Stream, 1975).

Wantagh
1. *Hempstead Inquirer,* April 7, 1838.
2. Seyfried, *Long Island Rail Road,* 1:78.
3. William S. Pelletreau and John Howard, *American Families of Historic Lineage, Long Island Edition* (New York: National American Society, n.d.), 2:581.
4. *Picket,* December 4, 1868.
5. Seyfried, Long Island Rail Road, 1:78.
6. *South Side Observer,* June 6, 1891.
7. Pelletreau and Howard, *American Families of Historic Lineage,* 2:581.
8. Fernow, *Documents,* 14:416.
9. Tooker, *Indian Place-Names,* p. 295.
10. *South Side Observer,* June 26, 1891; *East Norwich Enterprise,* July 4, 1891.
11. *South Side Observer,* October 2, 1981.
12. On the history of Wantagh, see Julian Denton Smith, "Wantagh Before Electricity," *Nassau County Historical Society Journal* 19 (Fall 1958): 13-24; Reprinted, ibid., 30 (1970) 11-21.

Westbury
1. Hicks, *Hempstead Town Records,* 1:300; *Westbury Times,* March 14, 1925.
2. Overton, *Long Island's Story,* p. 166; Hicks, *Hempstead Town Records,* 468.
3. *East Norwich Enterprise,* November 23, 1907.
4. *Picket,* April 10, 1868
5. Ibid.
6. *Long Island Democrat,* March 14, 1882; Seyfried, *Long Island Rail Road,* 3:188.

7. *Hempstead Sentinel,* December 22, 1908.

8. On the history of Westbury, see Sheila Lesnick, "The History of Westbury in the Twentieth Century" (M.A. thesis, Columbia University, 1981). A copy is in the Long Island Studies Institute, Hofstra University.

West Hempstead

1. Letter from Vincent F. Seyfried to the author, July 10, 1967.
2. Hyde, *Atlas of Nassau County,* 1914, p. 20.
3. Letter from Postmaster Arthur Folz, to the author, July 12, 1967.

Williston Park

1. *Westbury Times,* March 14, 1925.
2. Hicks, *Hempstead Town Records,* 1:150.
3. Seyfried, *Long Island Rail Road,* 3:203.
4. *Nassau Daily Review-Star,* October 24, 1951.
5. Meyer and Lewis, *East Williston History 1663-1978,* p. 26.
6. Ross and Pelletreau, *History of Long Island,* 3:183, 197. An East Williston Road Cart is in the Carriage House collections at The Museums at Stony Brook; a photograph and description can be found in [Merri Ferrell], *The Carriage Collection* (Stony Brook: The Museums at Stony Brook, 1986), p. 83.

Woodbury

1. Cox, *Oyster Bay Town Records,* 2:212, 679-80.
2. *Hempstead Inquirer,* August 10, 1836.
3. Cox, *Oyster Bay Town Records,* 8:91.
4. *Hempstead Inquirer,* August 10, 1836.
5. *Glen Cove Gazette,* May 8, 1858; *Hempstead Inquirer,* May 15, 1858.

Woodmere

1. Bellot, *History of the Rockaways,* p. 66.
2. Samuel Wood, *Woodsburgh, L. I., The New Summer Resort Showing the Origin, Location and Progress of This New Watering Place and the Plan Proposed to Encourage Settlement There* (New York: Privately printed, 1878), p. 3.
3. Bellot, *History of the Rockaways,* p. 66.
4. *South Side Observer,* October 15, 1897.
5. Ibid.
6. *Sea Cliff News,* March 19, 1892.
7. On the history of Woodmere, see references to the Five Towns under Cedarhurst, note no. 5.

Woodsburgh

1. Bellot, *History of the Rockaways,* p. 66.
2. *South Side Observer,* October 15, 1897.
3. Letter from Woodsburgh Village Clerk John F. Duncombe to the author, August 19, 1964.

Epilogue

1. Thompson, *History of Long Island,* 3d ed., 3:280-81. The quotation also appears in the 2d edition of the *History* published in 1843. Thompson was working on a revised and enlarged 3d edition when he died in 1849; it was published in 1918 with additions by Charles Warner.

Bibliography

Agins, Theodore C. *50th Anniversary, Incorporated Village of Kensington.* Kensington: Village of Kensington, 1959.

Aleph Zadik Alepha. *The First History of Oceanside.* Oceanside: First United Methodist Church, 1975.

Bailey, Paul, ed. *Long Island, A History of Two Great Counties, Nassau and Suffolk.* 2 vols. New York: Lewis Historical Publishing Company, 1949.

Bassett, Preston R., and Arthur L. Hodges. *The History of Rockville Centre.* Uniondale: Salisbury Printers, 1969.

Beauchamp, William M. *Aboriginal Place-Names of New York.* Albany: New York State Education Department, 1906.

Beers, F. W. *Atlas of Long Island.* New York: Beers, Comstock & Cline, 1873.

Bellot, Alfred H. *History of the Rockaways, From the Year 1685 to 1917.* Far Rockaway: Bellot's Histories, 1917.

Braner, Linda E. *The Mailman Cometh to Jericho.* East Hampton: East Hampton Star Press, 1960.

Braynard, Frank O. and Anthony Brescia, eds. *The Village of Sea Cliff, 100 Years.* Sea Cliff: Sea Cliff Centennial Commission, 1983.

Brodhead, John Romeyn, and E. B. O'Callaghan, eds. *Documents Relative to the Colonial History of the State of New York.* 14 vols. New York: Weed, Parsons and Company, 1856-1883.

Brown, Dorothy R. *Good Old Hicksville.* 5 vols. Hicksville: Privately printed, [1989-1992?].

Buczak, Stephen. *East Meadow, 1914-1950.* 13 looseleaf vols. North Bellmore: Stephen Buczak, 1989-1992. Available in the Long Island Studies Institute at Hofstra University.

Buhr, Jenni. "Levittown as a Utopian Community." In *Long Island: The Suburban Experience,* edited by Barbara M. Kelly, pp. 67-78. Interlaken, NY: Heart of the Lakes, 1990.

Cahn, Barbara F., ed. *An Illustrated History of Massapequa.* Massapequa: Massapequa Publishing Co., 1961; 2d ed., 1968.

Census of the State of New York for 1865. Albany: Charles Van Benthuysen, 1867.

Chapman Publishing Company, *Portrait and Biographical Record of Queens County, Long Island, New York.* New York: Chapman Publishing, 1896.

Christ, George E. *The Early History of New Hyde Park.* New Hyde Park: Privately printed, 1997.

Cobbett, William. *A Year's Residence in America.* Boston: Small, Maynard and Company, n.d. [1819?]. This book has been reprinted in different editions including by the University of Illinois in 1965.

Cocks, George William. "Old Matinecock." *Nassau County Historical Society Journal* 22 (Fall 1961): 1-11.

Coles, Robert R. *Glen Cove in the American Revolutionary War.* Glen Cove: Glen Cove Chamber of Commerce, 1976.

Coles, Robert Reed, and Peter Luyster Van Santvoord. *A History of Glen Cove.* Glen Cove: Privately printed, 1967.

Combes, George A. "The Naming of Hempstead." *Nassau County Historical Society* 29 (Summer/Fall 1969): 10-15.

Corey, Albert B. "Meaning of Schodack." *Long Island Forum* 20 (February 1957): 22.

Cow Neck Peninsula Historical Society Journal, 1965 to date.

Cox, John, Jr., ed. *Oyster Bay Town Records.* 8 vols. New York: Tobias A. Wright, 1916-1940.

DeKay, James Ellsworth. *Indian Names of Long Island Localities.* Oyster Bay: William L. Swan, 1920.

DeRiggi, Mildred. "The Settlement of Muskitoe Cove, 1668-1700." M.A. thesis, University of Delaware, 1979.

Deschin, Celia Spalter. *A Community Self-Portrait: The Five Towns as Seen Through the Eyes of Its Adult Residents, Its Adolescents, Health and Welfare Experts, and Its Community Leaders.* Typescript, 1965. A copy is in the Nassau County Museum collection, Long Island Studies Institute at Hofstra University.

Downing, Richard. *A Brief History of East Norwich, Long Island.* Syosset: Berry Hill Press, 1960.

Dwight, Timothy. *Travels in New England and New York.* 4 vols. London: William Baynes and Son, 1823. Reprint, edited by Barbara Miller Solomon. Cambridge: Harvard University Press, Belknap Press, 1969.

Earle, Walter K. *Out of the Wilderness.* Cold Spring Harbor: Whaling Museum Society, 1966.

East Meadow Public Library. *East Meadow: Its Past and Present, 1658-1976.* East Meadow: East Meadow Library, 1976.

Ehlen, Norma I. *This is Carle Place.* Carle Place: Carle Place Chamber of Commerce, 1958.

"Elmont's Our Home and We're Proud of It." Hempstead: Town of Hempstead, Department of Planning and Economic Development, 198?.

Evers, Richard E. *Hicksville Today and Yesterday.* Hicksville: Hicksville Public Schools, 1962.

———. *The Story of Hicksville, Yesterday and Today.* Hicksville: Privately printed, 1978.

Evers, Richard, and Anne Evers. "The Economic History of Hicksville." 4 vols. Typescript, spiral bound. Hicksville: Public Library 1988-1996. A copy is in the Long Island Studies Institute, Hofstra University.

Fernow, Berthold, ed. *Documents Relating to the Colonial History of the State of New York,* vol. 14, *Long Island.* Albany: Weed, Parsons and Company, 1883.

Ferrell, Merri. *The Carriage Collection.* Stony Brook: The Museums at Stony Brook, 1986.

Fiore, Roberta M. and Liz Coffin Allerhand. "Sand Bar to City: William H. Reynolds and the Planned Community of Long Beach 1906-1922." In *Nassau County: From Rural Hinterland to Suburban Metropolis,* edited by Joann P. Krieg and Natalie A. Naylor. Forthcoming from the Long Island Studies Institute and Empire State Books.

Flint, Martha B. *Early Long Island, A Colonial Study.* New York: G. P. Putnam's Sons, 1896. Reprinted under the title, *Long Island Before the Revolution; A Colonial Study.* Port Washington: Ira J. Friedman, 1967.

Foreman, Kenneth M. *A Profile of the Bellmores, With Historical Commentary and Background Information.* Bellmore: Bellmore Life and the Historical Society of the Bellmores, 1994.

French, J. H. *Gazetteer of the State of New York.* Syracuse: R. Pearsall Smith, 1860. Reprint; Baltimore: Genealogical Publishing, 1998.

Furman, Gabriel. *Antiquities of Long Island.* New York: J. W. Bouton, 1874. Reprint; Port Washington: Ira J. Friedman, 1968.

Gibbs, Alonzo. "Profile of a Long Island Town," (Valley Stream in the early 1920s). *Nassau County Historical Society Journal* 29 (Winter-Spring, 1969): 10-17.

Gibbs, Iris. "Building a School in 1878." *Long Island Forum* 11 (October 1948): 187, 194.

Gibbs, Iris, and Alonzo Gibbs. *Bethpage Bygones.* Bethpage: Kinsman Press, 1962.

———. *Harking Back.* Waldeboro, ME: Kinsman Publications, 1984.

Goddard, Conrad Godwin. *The Early History of Roslyn Harbor, Long Island.* Roslyn Harbor: Conrad Godwin Goddard, 1972.

Golden Anniversary of the Village of Stewart Manor, 1927-1977. Stewart Manor: Village of Stewart Manor, 1977.

Gordon, Thomas F. *Gazetteer of the State of New York.* Philadelphia: T. K. and P. G. Collins, 1836.

Gosden, Walter E., ed. *Floral Park 75th Anniversary, 1908-1983.* Np. 1983?

Hagedorn, Hermann. *The Roosevelt Family of Sagamore Hill.* New York: Macmillan Company, 1954.

Hagstrom Map Company. *Hagstrom Nassau County Atlas.* Maspeth: Hagstrom Map Company, 1992.

Hall, Courtney R. "Early Days in Hempstead, Long Island." *New York History* 24 (October 1943): 534-47.

Hallock, Lucius H. *A Hallock Genealogy.* Orient: Lucius H. Hallock, 1926.

Hammond, John E. *Crossroads: A History of East Norwich.* Np: Privately printed, 1997.

Hazelton, Henry Isham. *The Boroughs of Brooklyn and Queens, Counties of Nassau and Suffolk, Long Island, New York, 1609-1924.* 7 vols. New York: Lewis Historical Publishing Company, 1925.

Henry, Charlotte, compiler. "Hyde Park, Home of Long Island's Colonial Gentry (The Early Days of New Hyde Park)." Typescript photocopy, 1994. A copy is in the Long Island Studies Institute, Hofstra University.

Hicks, Benjamin D., ed. *Records of the Towns of North and South Hempstead, Long Island, N.Y.* 8 vols. Jamaica: Long Island Farmer Print, 1896-1904.

Hicks, Marietta. "Old Westbury and Jericho—A Closely Knit Quaker Community. Typescript, c. 1940. A copy is in the Nassau County Museum collection, Long Island Studies Institute at Hofstra University

Hicksville Tercentennial Committee. *Hicksville's Story, 300 Years of History 1648-1948.* Hicksville: Hicksville Tercentennial Committee, 1948.

Historical Society of the Massapequas. *Historical Society of Massapequa Celebrates the Anniversaries.* Massapequa: Historical Society of the Massapequas, 1981.

Historical Society of the Merricks. *Memories of the Merricks.* Merrick: Merrick Historical Society, 1977.

History of the Town of Hempstead: The 325th Anniversary. . . 1644-1969. Hempstead: Town of Hempstead, [1969?].

Horne, Field, ed. *The Diary of Mary Cooper: Life on a Long Island Farm, 1768-1773.* Oyster Bay: Oyster Bay Historical Society, 1981.

Hunt, [Harrison deF.] Terry/Terence S. [*sic*]. *Bethpage: The Years of Development, 1840-1910.* East Farmingdale: Oakdale Press, 1973, 1976.

Hyde, E. Belcher. *Atlas of Nassau County, Long Island, N.Y.* New York: E. Belcher Hyde, 1914.

——. *Real Estate Map of Nassau County, Long Island, N.Y.* New York: E. Belcher Hyde, 1923.

——. *Real Estate Map of Nassau County, Long Island, N.Y.* New York: E. Belcher Hyde, 1927.

"Indian Deeds, 1639, 1643, and 1657." In *Roots and Heritage of Hempstead Town,* edited by Natalie A. Naylor, pp. 173-77. Interlaken, NY: Heart of the Lakes Publishing, 1994.

Irvin, Frances. "Oyster Bay in History." Typescript, 1960. A copy is in the Long Island Studies Institute, Hofstra University.

Jameson, J. Franklin, ed. *Narratives of New Netherlands 1609-1664.* New York: Charles Scribner's Sons, 1910.

Janeske, Gerard J. *Malverne: The Story of Its Years.* Malverne: Incorporated Village of Malverne, 1972.

Johnston, William J. "Farmingdale's History: A Reflection of Nassau County's First Century." In *Nassau County: From Rural Hinterland to Suburban Metropolis,* edited by Joann P. Krieg and Natalie A. Naylor. Forthcoming from the Long Island Studies Institute and Empire State Books.

——. ed. "The World War II Homefront: The Farmingdale Experience." *Long Island Forum* 58 (Summer 1995): 18-35.

Jones, John H. *The Jones Family of Long Island, Descendants of Major Thomas Jones 1665-1726 and Allied Families.* New York: Tobias A. Wright, 1907.

Keller, Mollie. "Levittown and the Transformation of the Metropolis." Ph.D. diss., New York University, 1990. A copy is in the Long Island Studies Institute, Hofstra University.

Kelly, Barbara M. *Expanding the American Dream: Building and Rebuilding Levittown.* Albany: State University of New York, 1993.

——. "Levittown: Opening a New Frontier." *Nassau County Historical Society Journal* 47 (1992): 13-21.

Kent, Charles N. *An Historical Sketch of Merrick, Long Island, 1643-1900.* Merrick: Merrick Library, 1900.

Kling, Sandra Schoenberg. *A Demographic Profile of Hempstead Village, 1960-1985.* Hempstead: Hofstra University Center for Community Studies, 1985.

Koubek, Richard, compiler. *Our Town: Plainview-Old Bethpage Community Studies Resource Portfolio.* Plainview: Plainview-Old Bethpage Central School District, 1987.

Kreig, Joann P. "Barnum's Island, N.Y.: Fact or Fabrication." *New York Folklore* 10 (Winter-Spring 1984): 83-87.

——. ed. *Evoking a Sense of Place.* Interlaken, NY: Heart of the Lakes Publishing, 1988.

Krieg, Joann P., and Natalie A. Naylor, eds. *To Know the Place: Exploring Long Island History.* Rev. ed. Interlaken, NY: Heart of the Lakes Publishing, 1995.

League of Women Voters. *Hempstead Village, Yesterday and Today.* Hempstead: League of Women Voters of the Town of Hempstead, 1975.

League of Women Voters of Great Neck. *This is Great Neck.* Great Neck: League of Women Voters of Great Neck, 1995.

Lee, Henry J., ed. *The Long Island Almanac and Year Book, 1928.* Brooklyn: Brooklyn Daily Eagle, 1928.

Lesnick, Sheila. "The History of Westbury in the Twentieth Century." M.A. thesis, Columbia University, 1981. A copy is in the Long Island Studies Institute, Hofstra University.

Levine, Gaynell Stone, and Nancy Bonvillain, eds. *Languages and Lore of the Long Island Indians.* Vol. 4 of *Readings in Long Island Archaeology and Ethnohistory.* Stony Brook: Suffolk County Archaeological Association, 1980.

Liell, John. "Levittown: A Study in Community Planning and Development." Ph.D. diss., Yale University, 1952. A copy is in the Long Island Studies Institute, Hofstra University.

Long Island Association. *Long Island, The Sunrise Homeland, 1957.* 18th ed. Garden City: Long Island Association, 1957.

Long Island Rail Road. *Timetable,* October 1898.

Long Island Regional Planning Board. *Historical Population of Long Island Communities, 1790-1980.* Hauppauge: Long Island Regional Planning Board, 1982.

MacKay, Malcolm and Charles G. Meyer, *A History of Centre Island.* Np: Privately printed, 1976.

Manhasset Chamber of Commerce. *Manhasset: The First 300 Years.* Manhasset: Chamber of Commerce, 1980.

Manuscript of records in the Nassau County Clerk's Office, Mineola.

Maps on file in the Nassau County Clerk's office, Mineola, NY.

Marshall, Bernice Schultz. *Colonial Hempstead: Long Island Life Under the Dutch and English,* 1937. Reprint; Port Washington: I. J. Friedman, 1962. Published in 1937 under the name Bernice Schultz.

Matarrese, Lynne. *History of Levittown, New York.* Levittown: Levittown Historical Society, 1998.

Match, Richard. *Lucky Seven: A History of the Great Neck Public Schools.* Great Neck: Great Neck Public Schools, 1964.

Merle-Smith, Jr., Van S. *The Village of Oyster Bay, Its Founding and Growth From 1653 to 1700.* Garden City: Privately printed, 1953.

Merriman, Charlotte E. *Tales of Sint Sink.* Port Washington: Board of Education of Port Washington, NY, 1935. Reprint; Port Washington: Cow Neck Peninsula Historical Society, 1965.

Merritt, Jesse. Manuscript. In Nassau County Museum collections (Farmingdale vertical file), Long Island Studies Institute at Hofstra University.

Metz, Clinton E. *Freeport As It Was.* Np: Privately printed, 1976.

Meyer, Milton. *A Brief History of a Long Island Community Village of Lawrence.* Lawrence: Village of Lawrence, 1977.

Meyer, Nicholas A., and Cyril A. Lewis. *East Williston History, 1663-1978.* East Williston: Incorporated Village of East Williston, 1977.

Moger, Roy W. *Roslyn: Then and Now.* Roslyn: Roslyn Public Schools, 1965. 2d rev. ed. Edited by Myrna L. Sloam. Roslyn: The Bryant Library, 1992.

Mohan, Geoffrey. "Nassau's Difficult Birth." In Newsday, *Long Island: Our Story,* pp. 232-35. Melville: Newsday, 1998.

Moore, Rev. William H. *History of St. George's Church, Hempstead, Long Island, N.Y.* New York: E. P. Dutton & Company, 1881.

Morris, Joel J. "Hewlett Bay Park: The Hunting Club Connection." *Nassau County Historical Society Journal* 49 (1994): 15-26.

Mulvihill, William. *South Fork Place Names.* Sag Harbor: Brickiln Press, 1995.

Munsell, W. W. *History of Queens County, New York, With Illustrations, Portraits, and Sketches of Prominent Families and Individuals.* New York: W. W. Munsell Company, 1882.

Munsey Park Association. *Munsey Park at Manhasset.* New York: Munsey Park Association, n.d.

Nassau County Deeds. Microfilms in the Nassau County Museum collection in the Long Island Studies Institute at Hofstra University.

Nassau County Planning Commission. *Nassau County, New York, Data Book.* Mineola: Nassau County Planning Commission, 1985.

Naylor, Natalie A. "The Formation of Nassau County." *Nassau County Historical Society Journal* 53 (1998): 8-10.

——. ed. *The Roots and Heritage of Hempstead Town.* Interlaken, NY: Heart of the Lakes Publishing, 1994.

Newman, Estelle Valentine. "Cold Spring Harbor Hotels." *Long Island Forum* 13 (November 1950): 207-8, 218.

Newsday. *Home Town: Long Island.* Melville: Newsday, 1999.

——. "Levittown at Fifty." *Newsday,* Supplement, September 18, 1997, sec. H. Portions are included in Newsday, *Long Island: Our Story,* pp. 404-19. Melville: Newsday, 1998.

New-York Historical Society. *Abstracts of Wills on File in the Surrogate's Office, City of New York, vol. 4, 1744-1753.* In *Collections of the New-York Historical Society for the Year 1895.* New York: New-York Historical Society.

1912 Tax Roll, Village of East Rockaway, Long Island.

1922-1997, Long Beach: The Early Years. Long Beach: City of Long Beach, 1997.

1942-1943 Year Book of the Bay Park Property Owners' Association, Inc.

Nostrand, Doris , "Pronunciation, Geographical, and Historical Dictionary of Selected Place Names of Suffolk County, New York." M.S. report, C. W. Post Library School, 1971.

O'Callaghan, Edmund B., *History of New Netherland; or New York Under the Dutch,* 2 vols. New York: D. Appleton, 1848.

Onderdonk, Henry, Jr. *The Annals of Hempstead 1643 to 1832.* Hempstead: Lott Van De Water, 1878.

——. *Documents and Letters Intended to Illustrate the Revolutionary Incidents of Queens County, N.Y.* 2d series. New York: Leavitt and Company, 1846. Reprint; Port Washington: Ira J. Friedman Division of Kennikat Press, 1970.

——. *Queens County in Olden Times.* Jamaica: Charles Welling, 1865.

Oren, Allen. *This Old Town.* 12 videocassettes. Woodbury: News 12 Long Island, 1993.

Our Towns, A Bicentennial History. Hewlett: South Shore Record, 1976.

Overton, Jacqueline. *Long Island's Story.* Garden City: Doubleday, Doran and Company, 1929. 2d ed., with a Sequel, "The Rest of the Story, 1929-1961," by Bernice Marshall. Port Washington: I. J. Friedman, 1961.

Parker, Donald Dean. *Local History; How to Gather It, Write It, and Publish It.* New York: Social Science Research Council, 1944.

Pelletreau, William S. and John Howard. *American Families of Historic Lineage, Long Island Edition.* New York: National American Society, n.d.

Prime, Nathaniel S. *A History of Long Island, From Its First Settlement by Europeans, to the Year 1845, With Special Reference to its Ecclesiastical Concerns.* New York: Robert Carter, 1845.

Proehl, Karl H., and Barbara A. Shupe. *Long Island Gazetteer: A Guide to Current and Historical Place Names.* Bayside: LDA Publishers, 1984.

Queens County Deeds. Microfilm in the Nassau County Museum collection in the Long Island Studies Institute at Hofstra University.

Rawlinson, John Lang. *The History of Upper Brookville, 1932-1982.* Upper Brookville: Board of Trustees, [1982?].

Ross, Peter, and William S. Pelletreau. *A History of Long Island From Its Earliest Settlement to the Present Time.* 2 vols. New York: Lewis Historical Publishing Company, 1903.

Ruehl, Howard F. *History of Valley Stream, 1840-1975.* Valley Stream: Incorporated Village of Valley Stream, 1975.

Sammis, Romanah. *Huntington-Babylon Town History.* Huntington: Huntington Historical Society, 1937.

Sands Point Civic Association. *Sands Point.* Sands Point: Sands Point Civic Association, 1979.

Schultz, Bernice. *Colonial Hempstead, Long Island Life Under the Dutch and English.* Lynbrook: Nassau Daily Review-Star, 1937. See also Marshall, Bernice Schultz.

Scudder, Henry J. *An Address Delivered at Glen Cove, L.I., at the Celebration of the Second Centennial Anniversary of the Settlement of that Village.* New York: New York Printing Company, 1868.

Searingtown Methodist Episcopal Church. *150th Anniversary of the Searingtown Methodist Episcopal Church, 1785-1935.* Searingtown, 1935.

Secretary of State. *Manual for the Use of the Legislature of the State of New York for the Year 1849.* Albany: State Legislature, 1849.

Seyfried, Vincent F. *The Founding of Garden City, 1869-1893.* Garden City: Vincent F. Seyfried, 1969.

———. *The Long Island Rail Road, A Comprehensive History.* 7 vols. Garden City: Vincent F. Seyfried, 1966.

Shelley, Henry C. *John Underhill Captain of New England and New Netherland.* New York: D. Appleton and Company, 1932.

Shodell, Elly. *Flight of Memory: Long Island's Aeronautical Past.* Port Washington: Port Washington Library, 1995.

———. *Particles of the Past: Sandmining on Long Island in the 1870's-1980's.* Port Washington: Port Washington Public Library, 1985.

Sitterly, Glenn F. *The Illustrated Story of Baldwin, Long Island, N. Y. Through the Years.* Baldwin: Baldwin Union Free School District, 1984.

Smith, Julian Denton. "Wantagh Before Electricity." *Nassau County Historical Society Journal.* 19 (Fall 1958): 13-24; reprinted, 30 (1970): 11-21.

Smith, Mildred H. *Early History of the Long Island Railroad 1834-1900.* Uniondale: Salisbury Printers, 1958.

———. *Garden City, Long Island in Early Photographs 1869-1919.* New York: Dover, 1987.

———. *History of Garden City.* Manhasset: Channel Press, 1963. Reprint; Garden City: Garden City Historical Society, 1980.

Smits, Edward J. "Creating a New County: Nassau." *Long Island Historical Journal* 11 (Spring 1999): 129-44.

Spafford, Horatio Gates. *A Gazetteer of the State of New York.* New York: H. C. Southwick, 1813. Reprint; Interlaken, NY: Heart of the Lakes Publishing, 1981.

Spear, Devah, and Gil Spear. *The Book of Great Neck.* Great Neck: Privately printed, 1936.

Stewart, George R. *American Place-Names: A Concise and Selective Dictionary for the Continental United States of America.* New York: Oxford University Press, 1970.

———. *Names on the Land: A Historical Account of Place-Naming in the United States.* 2d ed. Boston: Houghton-Mifflin, 1967.

Stewart Manor Anniversary Committee. *Silver Anniversary of the Village of Stewart Manor 1927-1952.* Stewart Manor: Stewart Manor Anniversary Committee, 1952.

Stoutenburgh, Henry A. *A Documentary History of the Dutch Congregation of Oyster Bay, Queens County, Island of Nassau.* New York: Knickerbocker Press, 1907.

Strong, John A. *The Algonquian Peoples of Long Island From Earliest Times to 1700.* Interlaken, NY: Empire State Books, 1997.

Stryker-Rodda, Harriet. *Understanding Colonial Handwriting.* Reprinted from *New Jersey History.* Newark: New Jersey Historical Society, 1980.

Thomas, William S. "Incidents in Plandome History." *Nassau County Historical Society Journal* 11 (Autumn 1948): 17-23.

Thomaston Village. *Incorporated Village of the Village of Thomaston.* Great Neck, 1976.

Thompson, Benjamin F. *History of Long Island; Containing An Account of the Discovery and Settlement; With Other Important and Interesting Matters to the Present Time.* New York: E. French, 1839.

———. *History of Long Island From Its Discovery and Settlement to the Present Time.* 3d ed., revised and enlarged by Charles J. Werner, 1918. 3 vols. Reprint; Port Washington, NY: I. J. Friedman, 1962.

Tooker, William Wallace. *The Indian Place-Names of Long Island and Islands Adjacent, With Their Probable Significations*. New York: G. P. Putnam's Sons, 1911. Reprint; Port Washington: I. J. Friedman, 1962.

Tredwell, Daniel M. *Personal Reminiscences of Men and Things on Long Island*. 2 vols. Brooklyn: Charles Andrew Ditmas, 1912.

Tunison, Patricia A. *Looking Back on Syosset*. Syosset, 1975.

Tusiani, Beatrice. "A Complete History of Plandome Manor." Parts 1 and 2. *Long Island Forum* 44 (July/August 1981): 132-41, 168-73.

Upright, Carleton. *The Times and Tides of Bayville, Long Island, N. Y.* Bayville: Privately printed, 1969.

Valentine, Harriet G. *The Window to the Street: A Mid-Nineteenth-Century View of Cold Spring Harbor, New York, Based on the Diary of Helen Rogers,* 1981. Reprint; Cold Spring Harbor: Whaling Museum, 1991.

Van Allen, George R. *The Rise of Malverne*. Amityville: Long Island Forum, 1955.

Van Bloem, Kate. *History of the Village of Lake Success*. Lake Success: Incorporated Village of Lake Success [1968].

Van Pelt, Daniel. *Leslie's History of the Greater New York*. New York: Arkell Publishing Company, 1898.

Van Wie, Paul. *A History of Franklin Square and Environs: The Way It Was*. Franklin Square: Franklin Square Historical Society, 1994.

Village of Bellerose 50th Anniversary Committee. *Village of Bellerose 50th Anniversary Commemorative Album*. Bellerose: Village of Bellerose, 1974.

Vining, Dorothy H. *Farmingdale, A Short History*. Farmingdale: Farmingdale Public Schools, 1983.

Walton, Terry. *Cold Spring Harbor: Discovering History on Streets and Shores*. Cold Spring Harbor: Whaling Museum, 1999.

Watson, Elizabeth L. *The Houses for Science: A Pictorial History of Cold Spring Harbor Laboratory*. Plainview: Cold Spring Harbor Laboratory Press, 1991.

Watson, Floyd B. *History of Rockville Centre Public Schools and Some Early History of Rockville Centre*. Rockville Centre: Acorn Publishing Company, 1952.

Williams, George L. "The L.I.R.R. and Community Transportation—The Development of Port Washington 1900-1915." Parts 1 and 2. *Long Island Forum* 60 (Spring 1997): 4-16; and 60 (Summer 1997): 30-42.

——. *Lower Main Street: A Waterfront Community*. Port Washington: Landmarks Committee, Cow Neck Peninsula Historical Society, 1982.

——. *Port Washington in the Twentieth Century: Places and People*. Port Washington: Landmarks Committee, Cow Neck Peninsula Historical Society, 1982.

Willner, Steven J. *Lynbrook Legacy, The Story of Our Community*. Valley Stream: Maileader Publishing Corp., n.d.

Winsche, Richard. "History of the Place Names of Nassau County's Villages." M.A. thesis, Graduate Faculties, Long Island University (C. W. Post College), 1968.

Wood, Samuel. *Woodsburgh, L. I., The New Summer Resort Showing the Origin, Location and Progress of This New Watering Place and the Plan Proposed to Encourage Settlement There*. New York: Privately printed, 1878.

Writers' Program of the Works Projects Administration [WPA] in the State of New York. *Hick's Neck, The Story of Baldwin, Long Island*. Baldwin: Baldwin National Bank & Trust Company, 1939.

——. *The Story of the Five Towns: Inwood, Lawrence, Cedarhurst, Woodmere, and Hewlett, Nassau County, Long Island*. Rockville Centre: Nassau Daily Review Star, 1941.

———. *The Story of Roosevelt, Nassau County, Long Island,* typescript. A copy is in the Nassau County Museum collection (pamphlet file), Long Island Studies Institute at Hofstra University.

Newspapers

Babylon Town Leader, miscellaneous issues
Brooklyn Daily Eagle, miscellaneous issues
Brooklyn Daily Times, miscellaneous issues
East Norwich Enterprise, 1880-1925
Farmingdale Post, miscellaneous issues
Gateway (Floral Park), miscellaneous issues
Glen Cove Echo, miscellaneous issues
Glen Cove Gazette, 1857-1900
Glen Cove Plaindealer, 1852-1855
Hempstead Inquirer, 1830-1902
Hempstead Sentinel, 1900-1949
Levittown Tribune, miscellaneous issues
Long Island Democrat (Jamaica), 1835-1912
Long Island Farmer (Jamaica), miscellaneous issues
Malverne Herald, miscellaneous issues
Manhasset Mail, 1927-1962
Merrick Life, miscellaneous issues
Nassau County Review (Freeport), 1899-1905
Nassau Daily Review (Rockville Centre), 1921-1937
Nassau Daily Review-Star (Rockville Centre), 1937-1953
Nassau Daily Star (Lynbrook), 1927-1937
New Cassel Notes, miscellaneous issues
New York Daily News (New York City), miscellaneous issues
New York Herald Tribune (New York City), miscellaneous issues
New York Sun (New York City), miscellaneous issues
Newsday (Garden City/Melville), miscellaneous issues
North Hempstead Record (Manhasset), 1918
North Shore Daily Journal, miscellaneous issues
Oyster Bay Guardian, 1899-1940
Picket (Rockville Centre), 1865-1870
Plaindealer (Roslyn), 1850-1852
Port Washington News, 1903-1938
Queens County Review (Freeport), 1895-1899
Queens County Sentinel (Hempstead), 1858-1898
Roslyn News, 1878-1896
Sea Cliff News, 1883-1946
Southeast Nassau Enterprise (Wantagh), miscellaneous issues
South Side Observer (Rockville Centre), 1870-1920
Westbury Record, miscellaneous issues
Westbury Times, miscellaneous issues
Woodmere-Hewlett Herald, 1927-1931

Index

Page numbers in bold face type refer to the primary entry for the community.

M

Mackey, Elbert, 84
Macy, Carleton, 45
Madnank, 40, 51
Madnan's Neck, 40, 41, 51, 52, 91, 96
Mages, Mearck, 49
Mahican, 53
Malverne, 54, **61-62**, 108
Malverne Park Oaks, 108
Manetto, 47
Manetto Hill, 80, 81
Manhasset, 9, 33, 44, **62-63**, 68, 74, 81, 82, 84, 91, 108
Manhasset Hills, 108
Manhasset Indians, 63
Manhasset Isle, 63, 64
Manhasset Neck, 15, 34, 41, 96
Manhasset Valley, 63
Manhattan, 18, 48, 95
Manorhaven, **63-64**, 85, 108
Maple Hill farm, 89
Marietta, 60
Marospinc (Marossepinck), 65, 84
Marsh, Helen M., 18, 19
Marshfield, 29
Marten Gerritsen's Bay, 24
Martin, J. G., 97
Masepeage (Massapeage, Marsapeake), 64, 66
Massapequa, **64**, 65, 108
Massapequa Improvement Company, 64
Massapequa Park, **65**, 108
Matinecock (Matinneconcq/Matinnekonck), 25, 58, 59, **65-66**, 79
Matinecock Indians, 38, 40, 46, 52, 65, 98
McKee, Thomas, 84
Meadow Brook, 28, 98
Meadowbrook Estates, 28
Meadowbrook Farms, 28
Mechowodt, 84
Memphis, 60
Menioagamike, 68
Merriack, 66
Merrick, 11, 20, **66**, 74, 75, 86, 108
Merrick Indians, 66
Merryville, 47
Messepeake, 64
Methodist Meeting House, 85
Metropolitan Museum of Art, 68, 69
Meyers, Deputy Sheriff, 100
Middle Island, 25
Middletown, 27
Milburn, 15
Milburn Corners, 14
Milburn Creek, 14
Miller, John, 100
Miller, Philip J., 72
Mill Neck, **66-67**, 79, 108

Mill Neck Estates, 67
Millpond, 85
Millport, 62, 82
Mill River Neck, 67
Mineola, 8, 13, 23, 44, **67-68**, 108
Mineola Park, 23
Mitchell, Sidney Z., 66
Mitchell, Samuel Latham, 81
Mitchill, Robert, 81
Mitchill, Singleton, 62
Mohannis, (Hill, Cove), 26
Mollineaux, Royal, 87
Montauketts, 101
Morgan, E. D., 98
Morgan, Junius S., 66
Morris, H. Richard, 16
Morris, Walter A., 83
Moscheto Cove, 38
Moses, Robert, 22
Mosquetah, 38
Mosquito Cove, 38
Mott's Point, 92
Munsell, W. W., 99
Munsey, Frank A., 68-69
Munsey Park, **68-69**, 108
Munson, **69-70**, 103
Munson, Charles W., 34
Munson, Harry, 70
Musceata (Musketa, Musketo, Muskitoe), 38
Mutch, A., 48
Muttontown, 11, **70-71**, 108

N

Nassau-by-the-Sea, 83
Nassau Daily Review-Star, 83
Nassau Cottage and Realty Company, 83
Nassau County, 7-14, 18, 21, 28, 29, 110, 149; Division of Museum Services, 10, 149, 158
Native Americans, *see* Indians
Naylor, Natalie A., 9, 10
Near Rockaway, 16, 24, 29, 44, 48, 53, 56, 61, 85, 86, 99, 104, 105
Near Westbury, 102
New Cassel, **71-72**, 108
New Hyde Park, 8, 21, 32, 44, **72-73**, 75, 95, 108
Newark, 40
Newbridge, 20, 21, 73
Newington, 60
New Inlet, 83
Newtown, Town of, 28
New York City, 8, 17, 19, 21, 23, 36, 42, 49, 55, 56, 63, 96, 104
Nicoll, Matthias, 81
Nicolls, William, 81
Nissequogue River, 65

About the Author

Richard A. Winsche was born in a hospital in Jamaica, Queens, New York, but has been a life-long resident of Bellerose Terrace, Nassau County, New York. He attended the Floral Park-Bellerose School and Sewanhaka High School, both in Floral Park. In 1957, he graduated from Adelphi University, with a B.A. in history and government. In 1969, he received an M.A. in American history from Long Island University.

Richard Winsche was employed by the Nassau County Division of Museum Services in 1960 and served as a Curator and then as Historian, from 1968-1992. As historian for the Museum system he administered the museum's reference library and archival collections, researched and wrote reports on all historic sites and buildings administered by the County of Nassau, prepared forms for the National Register of Historic Places, and answered historical inquiries received by the county.

He is a long-time member of the Nassau County Historical Society and a life member of the Friends for Long Island's Heritage. He has written numerous articles for the *Long Island Forum,* the *Journal of Long Island History,* and the *Nassau County Historical Society Journal;* his writings have also appeared in *Long Island: The Suburban Experience,* edited by Barbara M. Kelly, and the forthcoming *Nassau County: From Rural Hinterland to Suburban Metropolis,* edited by Joann P. Krieg and Natalie A. Naylor, both books published by the Long Island Studies Institute through Heart of the Lakes Publishing.

The Long Island Studies Institute

The Long Island Studies Institute is a cooperative endeavor of Hofstra University and Nassau County. This major center for the study of local and regional history was established in 1985 to foster the study of Long Island history and heritage. Two major research collections on the study of Nassau County, Long Island, and New York State are located in the Special Collections Department on the University's West Campus, 619 Fulton Avenue, Hempstead, New York 11549. These collections—the Nassau County Museum reference collection and Hofstra University's James N. MacLean American Legion Memorial collection—are available to historians, librarians, teachers, and the general public, as well as to Hofstra students and faculty. Together, they offer a rich repository of books, photographs, newspapers, maps, census records, genealogies, government documents, manuscripts, and audiovisual materials.

In addition to its research collections, the Institute sponsors publications, meetings, and conferences pertaining to Long Island and its heritage. Through its programs, the Institute complements various Long Island Studies courses offered by the University through the History Department, New College, and University College for Continuing Education.

The Long Island Studies Institute is open Monday-Friday (except major holidays), 9-5 (Fridays to 4 in the summer). For further information, contact the Institute, 516-463-6411. The Institute also houses the historical research offices of the Nassau County Historian and Division of Museum Services (516-463-6418).

Long Island Studies Institute Publications

Heart of the Lakes Publishing/Empire State Books:
Aerospace Heritage of Long Island, The, by Joshua Stoff (1989).
Algonquian Peoples of Long Island from Earliest Times to 1700, The, by John A. Strong (1997).
Blessed Isle: Hal B. Fullerton and His Image of Long Island, 1897-1927, The, by Charles L. Sachs (1991).
Evoking a Sense of Place, edited by Joann P. Krieg (1988).
From Airship to Spaceship: Long Island in Aviation and Spaceflight, by Joshua Stoff (1991). For younger readers.
From Canoes to Cruisers: The Maritime Heritage of Long Island, by Joshua Stoff (1994). For younger readers.
History of Nassau County Community Place-Names, by Richard Winsche (1999).
Long Island Architecture, edited by Joann P. Krieg (1991).
Long Island and Literature, by Joann P. Krieg (1989).
Long Island: The Suburban Experience, edited by Barbara M. Kelly (1990).
Long Island Women: Activists and Innovators, edited by Natalie A. Naylor and Maureen O. Murphy (1998).
Making a Way to Freedom: A History of African Americans on Long Island, by Lynda R. Day (1997).
Nassau County: From Rural Hinterland to Suburban Metropolis, edited by Joann P. Krieg and Natalie A. Naylor (2000).

Robert Moses: Single-Minded Genius, edited by Joann P. Krieg (1989).

Roots and Heritage of Hempstead Town, The, edited by Natalie A. Naylor (1994).

Theodore Roosevelt: Many-Sided American, edited by Natalie A. Naylor, Douglas Brinkley, and John Allen Gable (1992).

To Know the Place: Exploring Local History, edited by Joann P. Krieg and Natalie A. Naylor (rev. ed., 1995).

"We Are Still Here!" The Algonquian Peoples of Long Island Today, by John A. Strong (1996; 2d ed., 1998).

Long Island Studies Institute:

Bibliography of Dissertations and Theses on Long Island Studies, by Natalie A. Naylor (1999).

Calderone Theatres on Long Island: An Introductory Essay and Description of the Calderone Theatre Collection at Hofstra University, The, by Miriam Tulin (1991).

Cumulative Index, Nassau County Historical Society Journal, 1958-1988, by Jeanne M. Burke (1989).

Exploring African-American History, edited by Natalie A. Naylor (1991, 1995).

To Know the Place: Teaching Local History, edited by Joann P. Krieg (1986).

Nassau County at 100: The Past and Present in Photographs, by Linda B. Martin (1999).

Greenwood Press:

Contested Terrain: Power, Politics, and Participation in Suburbia, edited by Marc L. Silver and Martin Melkonian (1995).

Suburbia Re-examined, edited by Barbara M. Kelly (1989).

The Institute collections and reading room are on the second floor of the Library Service Center on Hofstra's West Campus, 619 Fulton Avenue, Hempstead, NY.